D0829068

THE LITTLE BOOK OF BIG NETWORKING IDEAS

A GUIDE TO EXPERT NETWORKING

BY

NADIA BILCHIK

Bloomington, IN Milton Keynes, UK

AuthorHouse™
1663 Liberty Drive, Suite 200
Bloomington, IN 47403
www.authorhouse.com
Phone: 1-800-839-8640

AuthorHouse™ UK Ltd.
500 Avebury Boulevard
Central Milton Keynes, MK9 2BE
www.authorhouse.co.uk
Phone: 08001974150

This book is a work of non-fiction. Unless otherwise noted, the author
and the publisher make no explicit guarantees as to the accuracy
of the information contained in this book and in some cases, names
of people and places have been altered to protect their privacy.

First published by AuthorHouse 11/20/2006

ISBN: 1-4259-3767-5 (sc)

Library of Congress Control Number: 2006904163

Printed in the United States of America
Bloomington, Indiana
This book is printed on acid-free paper.

To Steve, Alexa and Julia
My network at home that makes all the rest possible

ACKNOWLEDGEMENTS

I want to thank my friend, mentor and colleague, Daphne Schechter, who saw the need for internal company networking within the Coca-Cola Company, and then worked with me to develop the Networking for Success program. Many of the ideas and concepts embodied in Networking For Success have become the inspiration for this book.

This book would not have happened without the skill and talent of Miriam Lacob Stix, who helped me translate every one of my seminars into readable sentences. Thank you for the hours spent researching every aspect of networking and for the late night calls and endless edits.

Thank you also to Suzanne Hanein, my dear friend, who helped me put together all the materials for my seminars when I first came to America. Without your knowledge, insight, and creative computer publishing skills, writing anything would still be a dream.

Special appreciation to the wonderful women I work with at the CNN Bookings Department, who demonstrate the benefits of mutually reciprocal networking on a daily basis.

And finally, thank you to Cliff Carle, whose organizational skills and discipline have kept us all on track and turned a manuscript into a book.

TABLE OF CONTENTS

INTRODUCTION

Whatever we have accomplished has been because other people have helped us.

— Walt Disney

There are people who are blessed with an organic network developed over a lifetime, consisting of the people they grew up with and went to school with—family members, playground friends, teachers, family acquaintances. But this is not always the case, particularly among young adults and people who are more mobile and adventurous. People move away from their original home for jobs, to improve their lives, and sometimes because they feel they have no choice. In my case, we moved from Johannesburg, South Africa, when my husband was offered the opportunity to join an exciting real estate start-up.

Americans are an especially mobile group of people. For example, the Census Bureau reports that between 2003 and 2004, 39 million people (or 14 percent of the population) moved. And Americans reportedly move an average of 11 times during their lives. Surveys have found that young adults have the highest moving rates, with the higher educated moving long distances for work. Those with a graduate degree or higher are most likely to have moved 500 miles or more.

If you have moved for employment reasons, you are not alone. In most cases, job-specific relocation is a pursuit for the young. One major moving company's annual Corporate Relations survey found that 93 percent of all transferees were between the ages of 25 and 45. Among the most highly mobile are business executives, who tend to make long-distance moves mostly for work related reasons.

Most people migrate to better their circumstances and take advantage of new opportunities—as embodied in the idea of seeking "greener pastures." But moving— whether it is changing cities, or simply starting a new job across town—can also be a real challenge. This is because it tears the individual away from his or her network of relatives and lifelong friends who provide valuable financial, health care, and many other types of support. Think of it like being a frequently repotted plant: mobility tends to disrupt social root systems. This kind of lifestyle presents individuals with the task of having to continually rebuild a network from the ground up.

MY PERSONAL STORY

I faced exactly that task when I moved from South Africa to Atlanta, Georgia with my family in 1997. We moved to take advantage of a once-in-a-lifetime opportunity to immigrate to the United States, for the stability and wonderful opportunities that this country offers. But it was not without pain, and loss. As a prominent television anchor in my home country, and with a thriving business, I had a brilliant career and an extensive, organic network of people, many of whom I had known all of my life.

I lost a lot in making the move—a beautiful home, close proximity to my parents, and a fabulous climate. Little did I know that one of the biggest losses of my move to the United States was the loss of my network, which extended back for generations. My grandfather came to South Africa from Russia in 1929. He founded a painting contract company called E. Bilchik and Co., and by the time I was born, Bilchik Wallpapers was a household name. I was therefore born into a network that extended from a lifetime insurance broker to the family doctor.

When I started my own communications company, On Cue, and I needed a loan for equipment, I had only to pick up the phone to my father's bank manager. Without so much as a signature, I had access to unlimited funds. When I left my car's hand brake off and it rolled into the neighbor's electricity pole, all I needed to do was call the family insurance broker, and my car was towed away and all the bodywork bills were paid. And when I started becoming a professional Media and Presentation Skills coach, all I needed to do was mention it to a high school friend, who had recently been appointed editor of a Sunday newspaper, and the promotional editorials flowed. Such is the power of an "organic network!"

As a newcomer to Atlanta I left all of that and more behind. I had the daunting task of building a completely new network from scratch. And now, every time I stand in front of a group of people at Turner Broadcasting (the parent company of CNN, Cartoon Network, and the Atlanta Braves, among others), Coca-Cola, Delta Technology, Accenture, or BellSouth, I remind each and every person that I would not be there if it was not for my ability to network.

It is not a process that has happened overnight. And it was not accomplished in some magical and mysterious way. It was achieved through hard work and the application of many commonsense networking strategies. It worked very well for me, and because of that, networking has become my passion.

The purpose of this book is to demonstrate that developing the highly effective networking skills, which I call "Expert Networking," is not mysterious or magical. Rather, it involves powerful, yet easy-to-learn strategies and approaches to relationships that you can make a part of your own skill set.

This book will take you step-by-step through the process of *Expert Networking*, and give you the opportunity to practice many of the practical strategies I am sharing with you along the way.

As you work your way through the book you will:

- Understand the true nature of networking.

- Analyze and overcome any of your own personal obstacles to networking.

- Develop a new paradigm of networking that can be transformational in effect.

- Learn to recognize potentially fruitful relationships.

- Practice transforming new interpersonal encounters from a connection to a conversation to a collaboration.

- Find and develop targeted networking opportunities.

- Become skilled at follow-up; and as an ultimate goal,

- Become a networking "go to" person—a truly powerful position to be in.

HOW TO USE THIS BOOK

In this book, I'm not just going to lecture to you. I'm going to invite you to:

1) Actively create your own tools for success.

2) Reflect on your own conscious and even unconscious behavior. It is this kind of awareness that will enable you to:

3) Develop and expand your network.

This will all be accomplished through self-reflection and diligently working on the series of exercises which are provided.

You can either read the book all the way through to get an overview, then come back and do the exercises—or, you can do the exercises as you come upon them.

Most of the exercises require some writing on your part. I will provide a space to write directly below the exercise. Some of you may prefer to write on separate sheets of paper, or in a journal. There will also be a section at the back of the book labeled "NOTES" which you can use for this purpose, or just to jot down random ideas that come to you. In many cases, you may need to reflect a little before responding to the exercises.

Equally, you may find that your responses will change as you go further down the road of expanding your network. It may even be helpful to make extra copies of the exercises, so that you can compare your earlier and later responses. And always keep in mind that the more diligently you participate in the exercises, the greater your results will be.

Chapter 1
What Is A Network?

We cannot live for ourselves alone. Our lives are connected by a thousand invisible threads, and along these sympathetic fibers, our actions run as causes and return to us as results.

— Herman Melville

The path to success in many fields begins with clear definitions. It is all very well talking about the importance of networking for life and career success, but it is a useless conversation without a clear understanding of what it means to have a network.

Having a social network means having a group of people who are sufficiently invested in you to have a stake in your well-being and success—and vice versa. It is important to note here that members of your network can be your friends and relatives, but not necessarily. More likely, it is the connections that you develop with people who are not close to you by virtue of blood ties or friendship that may be the ones with the biggest rewards. Either way, what's essential to *Expert Networking* is that you have found a way to make a *reciprocal* connection with this person, which will be to the advantage of *both* of you.

My relationship with the creator of the Coca-Cola Mentoring Program, Daphne Schechter, is a good example of this kind of mutually beneficial relationship. I met Daphne through a mutual friend. Daphne brought me into the Coca-Cola Company to teach a program on Intra-company Networking. She has become a wonderful champion, mentor and friend. Daphne recently left Coca-Cola to start her own company, and I have recommended her as a speaker and business consultant to several of my clients. We have also worked together to create a wonderful program on "Greater Impact Presentations," thus, the collaboration continues.

If you can visualize a telephone network, you will understand that networks are never unidirectional. *Expert Networking* is never a one-way street. It is vital to keep in mind that you have become part of a two-way, or even multidirectional process in which what you bring to the table becomes a vital element.

As networking guru Susan RoAne says, "Networking is a reciprocal process based on the exchange of ideas, information and knowledge, where resources are shared and acknowledged."

In the truest sense of the word, it means having a group of people who you invest in, care about, nurture and have at the top of the mind. These are people who will go the extra mile, and people who want to see you succeed—and always vice-versa! A true member of your network will take your resume to the head of marketing, rather than just directing you to a job website. But this person takes that step because he or she is certain that *you* would make a similar trip on his or her behalf.

Both of you are invested in a long-term connection, in which you have made a decision, or a commitment, to use your connections to help this member of your network throughout his or her life. This relationship is embodied in the unique ability to give of yourself in such a way that the person you are networking with feels sufficiently invested in your well-being. And so much so that they will trustingly and automatically try to move you forward in an effort to see you succeed. It could be for career, or it could be for your personal life; and that's what a network truly is.

The idea of "networking" is not new. As social scientist Bonnie Nardi points out, the term *networking*, as in cultivating useful others, has been in use since at least 1940. What is new, she emphasizes, and I agree totally, is "the intensity and absolute necessity of networking for practically everyone." And it will be pointed out over and over in this book that networking takes *effort*. Nardi and her colleagues have even dubbed it "NetWORK" in recognizing that successful people work hard at establishing and managing their personal and professional relationships.

WHAT ARE ITS ADVANTAGES?

Is NetWORK worth the effort? Definitely. Skillful and generous networking has been shown to be vital for career success. The social resources that people develop over time are known in the social sciences as "social capital." Researchers have found very strong links between social capital and career success, mainly because it facilitates access to social resources. These are, for example, access to hard-to-obtain information, business resources, and career sponsorship.

Indeed, studies of successful managers have found that they spend 70 percent more time networking and 10 percent more time communicating with the people they manage, or encounter in the course of their work, than their less successful counterparts. It is also a skill that helps you overcome a wide range of barriers, be they social or physical. As networking expert Rick Frishman points out: "In today's world, where the best people are protected by electronic fences and are impossible to reach, good networkers can get through and do so in a way that can get their targets to actually listen and act."

The ability to develop and maintain a personal social network is also an extremely adaptive response to the changing nature of the workplace, where old and set hierarchies and forms of organization are rapidly becoming obsolete. A group of anthropologists who studied personal social networks in the workplace concluded that they have become a key social structure for enabling work. This is because it is the "main form of social organization in the workplace as a dazzling new battery of communication technologies enables workers to connect to diverse, far-flung social networks."

Bonnie Nardi noted that because workers are no longer supported and nurtured by institutionalized group structure, they are being "increasingly thrown back on their own individual resources. Instead of being able to rely on various forms of teams and communities, access to labor and information comes through workers' own social networks—structures which they must carefully propagate and cultivate themselves."

In this kind of environment, individuals have much better control of their working lives if they become successful at creating and maintaining personal social networks. Unfortunately, it's not the kind of work you can put on a time sheet. Rather, networking is a kind of "invisible work" not accounted for in workflow diagrams or performance evaluations. But, smart workers know that they have to take it on so that they can do their jobs effectively and make the kind of progress they know they deserve.

If this all sounds very daunting, let me assure you that all your hard work will have a payoff that does not only come in career advancement. Social scientists like Nan Lin of Duke University have found that access to and use of the social resources that networks offer can lead to better socioeconomic status. It comes in terms of occupational status, more authority, a better position in certain industries, and of course, the size of your paycheck.

Why do you reap these benefits? Because you will have better and more timely access to information, and better access to financial and material resources, as well as higher visibility.

There is a further impetus for people to move beyond their own limited social circle. People who have ties outside of their social clique often have increased access to unique information and resources. Studies have shown that individuals who can access the information from the members of their social network, who are not close friends and relatives, are likely to have better information about job openings, and better access to contacts in other social groups. Similarly, an Academy of Management Journal study showed that individuals with multiple mentors reap greater career benefits than those having only one mentor.

Social networks are also good for our general well-being. Numerous studies have shown that having social support decreases the heart-racing, blood pressure boosting responses that human and other social animals have to stress.

One study of wild female baboons found that social mothers appeared to be better mothers. They found that the most social females enjoyed a reproductive success rate that was about one-third higher than the least social females, and that their infants have a higher survival rate.

Similarly, researchers at Ohio State University and Carnegie Mellon University have shown that people who report strong social supports have more robust immune systems and are less likely to succumb to infectious diseases.

Thomas Rutledge and his colleagues, who conducted research in San Diego, found that the women who had more social contacts and saw them more often also had lower blood glucose and blood pressure levels, and lower rates of smoking. Women with larger social networks also showed fewer signs of artery blockage during the four-year study. Not surprisingly, another study found that older men who have few personal relationships may have increased risk of heart disease.

Bonnie Erickson, a professor of sociology at the University of Toronto, reviewed research on people's social

On the Multiple Payoffs of Networking

Stephen's story: *Some years ago I was an executive at a magazine company. A young man called to ask if he could network with me and, as I almost always do, I told him I'd be happy to see him. We talked for about an hour or so, he sent the obligatory thank you note, and that was that.*

About six months later I received another note from him inviting me to a party to celebrate his new job. I went, and met an interesting young woman with dark, curly hair, and blue eyes with whom I spent most of the night talking. This same guy belonged to a group that rented a house in Westhampton over the summer, and he invited me to another party to meet the members of the group with the possibility of joining them. I went, and that same young woman — the one with the curls and the blue eyes — was there. We talked more, saw each other all summer, and about a year later were married.

There's still more. That new job the original networker landed was as an executive at a large communications company. He later invited me to join the company, which I did. So out of a simple act of agreeing to be a network source, I ended up with a place for the summer, my wife and a new job.

networks in several countries. She found that knowing many kinds of people in many social contexts improves one's chance of getting a good job, developing a range of cultural interests, feeling in control of one's life, and feeling healthy. In a study of participants in a Toronto social movement, she found that people with diversified general networks experienced less depression and were healthier.

As demonstrated by Stephen's story, on the previous page, these benefits can extend well beyond your working life. Researchers recently conducted a longitudinal study of retirees, and found that the most powerful predictor of life satisfaction right after retirement was the size of a person's social support network.

The study of social networks and the process of building "social capital" has become a respected field of academic study. Sociologist Nan Lin, who has quite systematically analyzed the advantages of building social networks, developed a theory of Social Resources. In her definition of social capital, she makes it clear that building a network is a form of investment. She goes on to say that the reciprocation is a vital part of the equation, because social capital is a form of "public good" that will fall apart if the individual members of the network become free riders. Lin defines social capital as "investment in social relations by individuals through which they gain access to embedded resources to enhance expected returns of instrumental or expressive actions."

Lin proposes several explanations as to why they are advantageous. For one, she notes, the flow of information is facilitated. "Social ties can provide an individual with useful information about opportunities and choices otherwise not available. Likewise, these ties… may alert an organization and its agents about the availability and interest of an otherwise unrecognized individual."

This information also makes it easier for organizations to recruit more skilled and better-qualified workers, and for employees to find organizations, which can use their "capital" and provide appropriate rewards. Social ties also help establish the credentials of an individual, and they also reinforce an individual's sense of identify and recognition.

"Being assured and recognized of one's worthiness as an individual and a member of a social group sharing similar interests and resources not only provides emotional support but also public acknowledgement of one's claim to certain resources. These reinforcements are essential for the maintenance of mental health and the entitlement to resources," Lin notes.

In summary, your network is, or will soon be, a group of people who care about you, and have a stake in your progress and success. Likewise, you will have a stake in theirs as well. The advantages are many, for all aspects of your life, including your career, social life, and a general sense of well-being.

CHAPTER 2
OBSTACLES TO CREATING A NETWORK

Commit yourself to a dream. Nobody who tries to do something great, but fails, is a total failure. Why? Because he can always rest assured that he succeeded in life's most important battle. He defeated the fear of trying.

— Robert H. Schuller

Most individuals are well aware that career and personal success depends in almost equal amounts on *who* you know, as well as *what* you know. Or as world-renowned management expert, Tom Peters, has commented, "It is what you know about who you know." But that does not stop most people from freezing and shutting down when faced with a networking opportunity, be it a company gathering or a town picnic.

As the savvy socializer Susan RoAne asks, "If working a room is so much fun and so profitable, why do our hearts thump, our palms sweat, and our eyes glaze over when we think about it?"

If this describes you, it is essential to delve deeply into what is stopping you. Ask yourself, "What is preventing me from investing in the people around me?" Or, "What is preventing me from becoming the kind of person who invests in another individual in such a way that makes them automatically want to reciprocate?"

It's true, some people avoid networking because they have been burned in some way by people who have taken advantage of them. But more people have subconscious obstacles blocking them from networking (or developing relationships) because of their negative perception of what networking is. In my networking skills classes that I have taught throughout the world, individuals express many of the same concerns and fears.

What are these fears? People tell me they are afraid of making a fool of themselves. Or they are afraid of speaking to strangers and being perceived as pushy. They fear rejection, lack confidence, can't spare the time, or are unsure of how to identify good environments in which to network. Yes, the obstacles can be expressed in all kinds of elaborate ways, but they all come down to *fear*. Fear is the prime factor, and "time" is the excuse.

Exercise: *Identifying your Conscious and Unconscious Obstacles to Networking*

At this time, you need to be totally honest with yourself. Try to identify the factors that hold you back from these three crucial networking activities:

Write down WHAT STOPS YOU FROM:

- Initiating a conversation with a stranger...

- Developing deeper and more reciprocal relationships with your co-workers and friends...

- Reaching out to potential mentors, employers and resources…

Do words like "uncertainty" and "fear" appear in your responses? These are common concerns, and that should be your first realization. Everybody experiences uncertainty and fear when faced with the unknown. In this case, it could be a person, or a group of people who you may not know at all, but who you need to get to know and hopefully develop a relationship with. If this is a frightening prospect, it may be helpful to realize that fear of rejection is very deep seated. In fact, a study of the brains of individuals who were subjected to rejecting situations revealed that this experience activated the same part of the brain that is involved in physical pain. The scientists who reported this research theorized that this link developed because social relationships are so important to an individual's survival.

Therefore, if your goal is to approach a group of strangers without feeling, at least, the fear of rejection, then you are not being realistic. Rather, it is important to recognize that you are experiencing a normal response to a personally challenging situation. And it may help to remember the words of John McCain: "Courage is not the absence of fear; it is taking action despite the fear."

CHANGING THE PARADIGM

How many times have you come home from a business or social event with a pocket full of business cards and no intention of ever calling one of them? The first step to overcoming your own personal obstacles to networking is to realize that it is time to revise and reframe your definition of networking. This will help you develop an entirely new approach and attitude that has the added advantage of addressing many of the concerns you may have. So, the first step toward revising your definition of networking is to review a list of what it is not.

Networking Is Not:

- Thrusting yourself or your card in front of as many people as possible

- Meeting and greeting as many people as you can

- Giving your "elevator speech" in 20 seconds so that someone will "buy you"

- Only targeting people who you think can do something for you

- Developing a gigantic database of names

- Something that is short term

- Only about promoting yourself

- Picking somebody up

- Instant rapport

- Love at first sight

Exercise: *Recognizing Those Networking Turnoffs*

An exercise that would be helpful right now is to list the reasons why you have not followed up with most of the individuals who have thrust a card into your hand.

- Were they too pushy?

- Did they move too fast?

- Ask too much of you too soon?

- Make promises that they could not keep?

Write down some of your reasons here, or on a separate sheet of paper:

Now, take a look at this list. You may recognize that many of these actions have one element in common: They are essentially selfish and one-sided activities.

This leads us to the most important element of your new approach to *Expert Networking*:

If you change your paradigm of networking from an activity valued for what you can GET out of it, to an activity that delivers its rewards based on what you can GIVE to it, you will be well on your way to success.

Chapter 3
Become a "Go-Giver"

The Universe operates through dynamic exchange;
giving and receiving are different aspects of the flow
of energy in the universe. And in our willingness to
give that which we seek, we keep the abundance of
the universe circulating in our lives.

— Deepak Chopra

Instead of being a so-called "go-getter," one of the most powerful networking tools you can develop is to become a "go-giver." So often you go into a situation focused on what you can get out of it immediately, rather than what you can give. This kind of attitude can be detrimental because *Expert Networking* is as much about *giving* as it is about getting. Think of it as making a long-term deposit in the Favor Bank of Life, and rewards will follow. Because, when you give or offer advice, or provide leads, the recipient will likely feel an automatic investment, and a desire to return the favor.

This is not just about the Biblical decree, "It is better to give than to receive." It's about developing the kind of attitude that says a lot about the kind of person you are.

"Go-Giving" In Action

For a clearer idea of how becoming a "Go-Giver" can help overcome your own inhibitions about networking, consider the following example:

I recently gave a class at the Turner Broadcasting Professional Development Center where Brian, one of the attendees, worked for the Atlanta Braves. At the start of the class, Brian said he always found networking difficult because he hated to be "needy" or to ask for a favor.

A couple of weeks after the class, he related to me how changing the paradigm had helped him. Instead of approaching a potential new employer with a "What can you do for me?" attitude, he went into the interaction thinking, "I am in a great position to be helpful to you. I am young, enthusiastic and energetic. I am also eager to benefit from your many years of experience in the field." In communicating both his energy and willingness to learn from his potential new employer, he realized that by asking

for advice or guidance he was "giving" the potential employer respect and acknowledgement.

Being helpful to the other person does not always need to be a concrete action. You can be equally helpful by acknowledging the other individual's achievement, and giving him or her a chance to offer advice. For example, a question framed as follows: "Mr. Smith, you have been very successful in navigating the world of sports management; do you have any ideas on how I should proceed?" recognizes his success by respecting his input and opinions. (Note: this approach is not a demand, but a request.)

Keep in mind that networking is a privilege, *not* a right. Networking author Rick Frishman emphasizes that this attitude should become a way of life, not an "occasional tactic." He states that it is vital to establish a wide reputation as a person who is genuinely eager to help out and not simply to set up others to get something in return. It's learning to be selfless, to be helpful and generous.

Of course, like any investment, the payback might take time, but it will come, one way or another. What you are working on is a long-term, hopefully lifelong connection. And it could even have an effect on your longevity.

A recent University of Michigan study found that older people who are helpful to others reduced their risk of dying by nearly 60 percent compared to peers who did not provide help or emotional support to relatives, neighbors or friends.

I, myself, have truly experienced the rewards of generous, patient networking as illustrated in the following experience:

As a new arrival in Atlanta, I signed up with a formal networking group to meet people and make contacts. While I never got any leads that turned into a job, I did meet a friend, Kate, who had a freelance marketing company at the time. After a year we both decided to leave the group but we continued to meet regularly for lunch. During one of these lunches, Kate mentioned that she had just met Nancy, the president of a communications company who hired external consultants, and she arranged for us to meet.

At the time, Nancy was working on a book and did not have any immediate work. She did, however, mention that her son, who had lived in Mexico, was interested in broadcast journalism.

I volunteered to meet with her son, to see if I could provide any guidance. After meeting with her son, I offered to pass his resume on to Eric, a colleague of mine at CNN International, who was responsible for hiring writers. I also gave him my advice on what was required, and an excellent book on broadcast journalism. Of course it helped that he was a skilled and talented writer. He was hired, and is thoroughly enjoying his career in the CNN newsroom.

Eventually, Nancy did have an opportunity for me and I have continued to work for her as a presentation skills trainer ever since. Nancy is now an essential member of my network. We are two people who are mutually invested in each other's success. The fact that I went "out of my way" to assist her son helped to consolidate this. My friend, Kate, who made the first contact, remains an integral part of this network. Both Nancy and I feel indebted to her for the introduction and we continue to look out for marketing opportunities for her burgeoning business.

In this regard, a question I am often asked is, "I can certainly give to someone who needs something I have to offer. But how do I 'give' to someone who does not need me?" Or, "How do I 'give' to someone whose expertise, advice, or contacts I need?" The answer is simple: Giving comes in many forms.

Exercise: What do YOU have to Give?

A useful strategy is to develop a self-inventory to determine what you bring to the table for your network. This includes your talents, natural attributes, skills, acquired capabilities, values and objectives that you consider important. For example, Benjamin, an ambitious young college graduate starting out in the working world, could list his attributes as:

- Smart

- Energetic

- Resourceful

- Flexible, and

- Available.

He approached a high-powered executive, and offered to document the company history in exchange for mentoring. As a result, Benjamin had access to each and every person in the company, and interviewed many of them. With this kind of access, he was able to learn about a vacancy in the company, and lobby successfully for the job.

So, what do YOU bring to the table (Or, the organization, group, forum or committee that you want to join)?

To complete this exercise, to the right of each word you wrote, give an example of an instance where you were able to successfully apply this attribute.

RESPECT AND ACKNOWLEGMENT

As previously mentioned, you can also "give" to someone by showing respect for their guidance. Most people are very willing to share their wisdom if the question is framed in a way that acknowledges them. This gives the other person recognition, and validates their success.

Experiment with these questions, rephrasing them for your situation:

- "Mr. Wilson, you have been so successful in positioning yourself in the company; I am at a crossroads, how do you suggest I proceed?"

- "Jeanette, you have navigated your career with great success; do you have any suggestions for me, starting out?"

I have also learned in the world of networking (as in the case of Nancy) that while the president of an organization or the head of a department may not need your help, he/she may have a son/daughter/niece/nephew who does.

How do you find out this information? The answer comes from the old pro Dale Carnegie: "You can make more friends in two weeks being interested in other people, than in two years trying to get them interested in you." Take time to connect with people, and work at becoming a great listener and a good conversationalist. Ask a lot of questions about *them* (their outside interests, their passions, and of course, their family). Afterwards, make sure that they know who you are, and what you do, and that you are open to assisting them in any way that you can.

CHANGE THE RADIO STATION

For your mind to work like an *Expert Networker*, you are constantly thinking every time somebody says something to you. You're thinking, "What can I do? How can I help? What resources do I have?"

Instead of being constantly tuned into WIFM (What's In it For Me), you change your radio station to WIBU (What's In it for Both of Us?)

I was once asked to lunch by a young woman who wanted to talk to me about media training. Without taking a breath, Heather asked me how she could get started, how I got my clients, and what should a training session consist of. At no point during the discussion did she offer me anything in return for my "intellectual property." Had she been more astute in the art of networking, Heather would have said, "Nadia, you are an experienced media trainer, but I have lived in Atlanta all my life. If I find us the clients, would you like to partner with me?"

You see, Heather has the vast Atlanta database, and is very well connected. She didn't leverage that. Instead she came across as a pushy, WIFM/WCIU (What's In it For Me, Where Can I Use you) person. She demanded rather than requested, and as a result she alienated a potential source of information, resources and possibly work.

DO TRY IT AT HOME

If you want to test this new paradigm before you launch into *Expert Networking*, try it at home, or better yet, with a friend.

Exercise: *Becoming a Strategic Resource*

Find a cooperative friend or acquaintance who has not up until now been part of your network. In classes when we have practiced this exercise, people have found everything from new jobs, to housekeepers; someone even found a doctor to do her plastic surgery.

Brainstorm with each other. The following are some useful questions to start:

- What do I know?

- What do I have?

- Who do I know?

- Who is in my network already?

- How can they be helpful to this "new" member of my network?

Remember: *Networking* **is about giving, sharing and caring. It is as much about being a go-giver as a go-getter.**

Chapter 4
Overcoming Networking Obstacles

Perseverance is a great element of success: If you only knock long enough and loud enough at the gate, you are sure to wake up somebody.
— Henry Wadsworth Longfellow

"I can't!" or "I'm not naturally good at it!"

That's what most people say when they describe their networking abilities. Many people believe networking is innate, that you either are born with the ability to talk to people or you aren't. But skill in networking is not the result of a gene. It is a skill that can be learned and honed. Networking is more like gardening: you read about it, you think about it, you plan and then you practice. Moreover, just like gardening, networking can be learned and perfected. Think of networking like planting a "relationship seed." If properly planted, and carefully nourished with time and attention, it will flourish. And, like cultivating a garden, keep in mind that after the seed is planted, the network takes time to build, and that seeds that receive too little water and fertilizer will probably die.

OVERCOMING YOUR FEAR OF REJECTION

"I'm afraid of approaching strangers."

Have you ever said this? Or thought this? Many of us fear approaching strangers, initiating conversations, or calling people in our network because we anticipate rejection. These kinds of concerns are entirely understandable because our psycho-physiological makeup is such that we do everything in our power to avoid pain. And rejection is just that: Pain. In fact, as noted previously, studies have located the sites of the brain where individuals experience physical pain as the same sites where an individual experiences the psychological pain of interpersonal rejection.

It is human nature to want to prevent oneself from experiencing pain. On a subconscious level we avoid situations that expose us to feelings that cause discomfort. For most people, this is the greatest inhibitor in reaching out and building new relationships.

Consider: How many times have you stopped yourself from making a connection based on one or more of the following questions:

- "What if the person is not interested?"

- "What if they do not return my call?"

- "What if they turn away when I approach them?"

These are absolutely normal fears. Nobody wakes up and says, "Please expose me to pain." Consciously or unconsciously, you are conditioned to avoid situations that may cause discomfort. As the renowned life coach, Anthony Robbins, has pointed out, 99% of people are paralyzed by fear. So, the key to *Expert Networking* is to join the one percent of people who have overcome their fear.

The same principle applies to approaching a stranger, arranging a meeting, or going to a networking function. It is vital that you recognize the urgency of exposing yourself to those situations, because the benefits far outweigh the disadvantages.

You do not have to be an extrovert to be an *Expert Networker*, but you do have to be willing to take risks, and cope with possible rejection. As Susan RoAne points out: "You'll never know if the person sitting next to you could change your life if you don't speak to them." Or, as Rick Frishman puts it: "You might be standing in line next to your future husband or the person who will give you your next job. Call it luck, call it fate, but you can't call it anything if you don't open your mouth and say hello."

To look at it another way: if you don't even try, *you* just rejected yourself. *That* should be your biggest fear. And while you're at it, commit to memory these powerful words by Eleanor Roosevelt: "No one can make you feel inferior without your consent."

It is also important to recognize that networking relationships do not have to develop into deep and lasting friendships. If anything, a wide variety of informal acquaintances can be more professionally advantageous. Sociology professor Bonnie Erickson, who studies social networks, found in one study that individuals who had a wide diversity of acquaintances were often more successful. Employees with more network variety got jobs with higher rank and higher income. The reason for this, she notes, is that "acquaintances are more varied, less like each other, and more likely to have new information, and more likely to include people highly placed enough to influence hiring.

"Thus family and close friends provide fewer jobs than do people outside the intimate circle. More highly placed people generally have connections to higher-placed jobs. An advantage of having varied connections is an improved chance of knowing such a useful contact. Another advantage of diversified connections is their value to a future employer, who often wants people with varied connections that the firm can use."

Moreover, like a high diver who takes a deep breath before taking the plunge, there are strategies that you can utilize to both recognize and transcend your fears.

Is Your "Inner Child" Talking?

One way to overcome feelings of rejection is to recognize that we can all have deep-seated "inner child" reactions to social situations that involve rejection or conflict. Kip Williams is an Australian psychologist who specializes in the psychology of ostracism and rejection, and even he found himself experiencing that pain:

"I was at a park with my dog and suddenly a Frisbee rolled up and hit me in the back. I took it and looked around and there were two guys playing, so I threw it back to them thinking that I'd go back to my dog. But then they threw it back to me. So then I threw it to them and they threw it to me, so I sort of joined their group and we were throwing it around for a couple of minutes. And then, all of a sudden they stopped throwing it to me and they just threw it to each other back and forth and back and forth. I was amazed at how bad I felt so quickly, and I also felt really quite awkward. Finally I just sort of slithered back to my dog, and if it weren't for the fact that I was a social psychologist, I think I would have felt worse still."

Williams was experiencing that "nobody wants to play with me" pain, which we all probably were exposed to at some point in our childhood. His strategy for overcoming the pain was to adapt the experience for use in the laboratory by measuring an individual's neural response to the perceived experience of being excluded from a game. Our response as adults embarking on the road toward *Expert Networking* is to remind ourselves that it is our inner child that fears rejection. We, on the other hand, are grown-ups, and have probably already survived numerous and varied experiences of rejection already. It is always the inner child that is concerned that perhaps "no one wants to play with me." But as adults we have the ability to rationalize and counsel ourselves. The worst that can happen is that you will hear the word "no." But as adults we have the skill and ability to not take it personally.

Exercise: *Recognizing Your "Inner Child" Reactions*

An important first step to overcoming "Inner Child" reactions is to become aware of them. In the following exercise, circle the response (A, B, or C) that best describes the action you would normally take in the various situations.

1) You are shopping in a crowded supermarket and discover that another shopper has walked off with your cart. Would you...

   A) Rush up to the shopper and demand the return of your cart?

   B) Simply point out to the shopper that she has taken your cart, and acknowledge that she made an understandable mistake in the crowded supermarket?

   C) Offer to help the shopper find her own cart and while you are both looking, start a conversation about the difficulties of shopping for groceries on the weekends?

2) You are at a school function and notice an empty seat at a table. Most of the people at the table appear to know each other already. When you take the empty seat, the other people at the table carry on with their conversations. Would you...

A) Clam up, feel miserable, and count the minutes to the end of the event?

B) Decide that this group of parents is clearly not interested in newcomers, get up, and go in search of somewhere else to sit?

C) Pick up the plate of cookies on the table, and offer them around?

3) You and a colleague are the leading candidates for a new position. The colleague gets the promotion instead of you. Would you...

A) Feel deeply humiliated and lay low for the next week?

B) Let other co-workers know that you felt the decision was unfair to gauge their reactions?

C) Make a point of congratulating your colleague, and offering your support?

Where do you stand?

If you identified more closely with 'A' responses, then your "Inner Child" is doing most of the reacting for you, and you will need to work a little harder on your networking skills. If you picked mostly 'B' responses, your networking techniques are developing, but could do with more honing. If you picked mostly 'C' responses, you are well on your way to being an *Expert Networker.*

Exercise: *Talking to Your Inner Child*

When somebody does not treat you in the way you would like to be treated, or if someone is not friendly or you feel that you have been unfairly treated, that's when you have to remind yourself that you feel on some level that it is almost as if *nobody wants to play with you.* You have to remember you are an adult, and have the ability to dialogue with yourself.

Think about a time in the last couple of weeks when you were upset or irritated, or felt in some way you were dismissed or rejected.

What kinds of feelings did you have?

Can you identify the "Inner Child" feelings that have been evoked? Are they:

- Someone stole my toy!

- Nobody wants to play with me!

- They didn't choose me for the game!

- They're picking on me!

- They're laughing at me and calling me names!

- But I didn't break the vase or spill the milk!

- It's not fair!

Now that you have identified your "inner child" response, you can, as an adult, dialogue with yourself, and write down a more "adult" reaction. Remember, you are a grown person with the gift of having the ability to take the initiative, and if necessary, the power to walk away from an unpleasant situation without taking it personally.

Make a note of your more adult reaction here:

DON'T TAKE THINGS PERSONALLY

In *The Four Agreements*, the Toltec sage, Don Miguel Ruiz, writes that we shouldn't make assumptions and shouldn't take things personally: "Nothing others do is because of you," he writes. "What others say and do is a projection of their own reality, their own dreams. When you are immune to the opinions and actions of others, you won't be the victim of needless suffering."

While Ruiz calls this an assumption, a more conventional psychologist would call it *projection*. We project our feelings and beliefs onto other people. So, in the case where you are treated rudely or dismissively by an individual you are trying to get to know, it is natural to assume that the person is reacting to you. However, it is frequently the case that this unfriendly, cold, or frankly rude individual is caught up in his or her own thoughts, feelings or problems. One useful strategy in these kinds of situations is to say to yourself, "happy people are nice, and unhappy people are unkind!" I even go so far as to tell myself that someone who was unresponsive to me may be in terrible pain.

I have so inculcated this into my children, that if someone at school is nasty to them, they frequently express more concern about the emotional state of the child who has treated them badly than their own hurt feelings.

Realizing the extent to which people who are cold and rejecting are often expressing their own negative feelings can enable you to achieve a necessary distance from this kind of challenging interpersonal situation. Ask yourself: "What's the worst that could happen?" Although our inner child may be wounded and feel like "the other child does not want to play with me," or "they don't like me," the advantage of being an adult is the capacity to realize that "it is not about me."

As you change your paradigm, you'll start realizing that if you don't get the desired response, it's not necessarily personal.

Once you understand that the pain of fear is a factor for most people, except for the very few who acknowledge it, you will be able to dialogue with yourself and take action despite the fear. If you do that you will be amazed at how much easier it is to remove the fear. Moreover, if you do not take rejection personally, you will find it easier to perceive the situation differently, and therefore open yourself up to countless networking opportunities.

MOTIVATE YOURSELF TO MOVE FORWARD

There's an old saying: "He who wants milk should not go to the pasture and *wait* for the cow to back up to him." Besides overcoming the fear factor, there is another consideration. Surely everyone is familiar with another popular saying: "Nothing ventured, nothing gained." This is an attitude that will certainly help you on the road to *Expert Networking.* Yes, rejection and pain is a possibility. But it is negligible if you make the calculation of what you would lose if you don't initiate the conversations, and develop the relationships. Surely the pain of never getting the job opportunity is greater than the fear of calling? Ask yourself, "What do I have to lose by reaching out compared to the potential gains?" Remember, if you ask for something, you may not always get what you want. But if you don't ask at all, you absolutely won't get it.

Use the promise of success and the future benefit to motivate yourself to take chances. You will find that there will sometimes be rejection, but there will also be plenty of acceptance. And there's another thing to keep in mind: you only need one parking place, one job, and one spouse at a time. In other words, relax. You don't need to become everyone's best friend, and feel the pressure to have a meaningful interaction with everybody you meet.

Another useful strategy is to be honest with yourself. There isn't a magic formula that you can apply and suddenly you'll stop being fearful. There's not going to be some magic wand that's waved over you and suddenly you shout, "NOW I'M A BRAVE PERSON." It doesn't happen like that. Rather, you can become a person who can take a little more pain. You can tell yourself: "I don't love doing this, but I'll deal with it. Because that's what is going to take me to the next level." The important point is it is easier to *act* your way to feeling better, to temporarily put on the mask and do what it takes to be proactive, than it is to change the way you feel about new social interactions.

Keep in mind as well that overcoming fear will be its own reward, because as you start to feel better about yourself as a proactive rather than passive person, you will be ever more ready to take on more challenges. And, yes, you will be less reticent about speaking to strangers who could become potential resources.

Always Speak to Strangers

Bill's Story: *While waiting for an appointment in the lobby of a large food service company, I introduced myself to James, a salesman who was also in the lobby. I learned that he was demonstrating his blenders to 70 food service representatives at an upcoming sales meeting. I asked what product he was going to use and he said he hadn't decided yet. I offered the use of my company's mixers if he would be willing to pass out a flyer. Instead, he invited me to give a talk to the representatives myself, giving me a lot of valuable exposure, and also saving me the company fee. In the future, James intends to use my company's mixers when demonstrating his blenders. He said he would gladly pay for them and he will pass out a flyer for the mixers when doing so. If I hadn't made the effort to introduce myself to a stranger, this would not have happened.*

It's Not About Being Pushy

Networking is only perceived as pushy if you believe networking is strictly about receiving. I challenge you to develop the mindset that *Expert Networking* is more about *giving*. And it is more about *contributing* in some way, whether small or large, to the people who you connect with. Not only is it better to Give than to Receive, as the Bible says, but it is also easier on your ego. Most people feel more comfortable if they are in a position of giving a favor, rather than asking for one.

So why is it about giving? Well, what happens when you give? You are in the driver's seat; you become the resource, the person who holds the power, the *go-to* person, someone people need to know. You become a worthwhile investment. You can only be perceived as pushy if you are only in this pursuit for yourself. Susan RoAne calls this type of person a "networking mongrel." Once you understand that *Expert Networking* is a form of *mutual* interaction, you'll learn to frame requests and approaches in a way that is not perceived as pushy.

How To Be in the Driver's Seat

- Request rather than demand access to people.

- Do not limit your networking to people who you perceive as powerful. (Or you will quickly get the reputation for being selfishly expedient.)

- If you are in a conversation, don't scan the room for the next person to approach.

- Walk into your relationships generously. (There are people who try to claw their way to the top, and these kinds of people may get ahead, but they rarely stay ahead.)

- Approach people without invading their personal space. (Give them room to breathe.)

- Don't make requests before you begin to understand a person and forge a solid connection.

- Don't offer more than you can deliver, or feel comfortable delivering.

- Don't be too attached to the outcome. (This increases your anxiety and undermines your confidence.)

- Take it slowly. (Show that you have patience.)

To expand on the last item, your best relationships are those that have been built slowly over time. You don't have to be a social butterfly. Sometimes I'll go to an event and just sit at a table. I don't run around the room trying to meet people. I simply sit at my table and see what results from having interaction with the few people sitting nearest me.

Similarly, I have walked into cocktail parties where there are fifty people. I never try to meet all of them. I will talk to and create a relationship with one person, and maybe two, but I will feel no urgency and I will not go into that room with a sense of pressure. I do not do the "card thrust," because I know that meeting fifty people is meaningless. The only thing that's meaningful is the person who you happen to connect with.

Another very effective strategy that has the advantages of both helping to overcome your fear of approaching strangers, and putting you in control of the situation, is to think of every situation as if you were the host of your own party. Take charge and take the initiative. If you were hosting your own party you wouldn't wait for introductions to be made. You would try to make sure all of your guests feel more comfortable. How? You would facilitate conversations. You'd introduce one guest to another. You would do your best to make sure everyone was feeling relaxed and enjoying themselves.

Remember, most people feel exactly the same way you do. But you have the advantage of being more conscious of the *Expert Networking* process.

STARTING A CONVERSATION

Don't knock the weather; nine-tenths of the people couldn't start a conversation if it didn't change once in a while – Kin Hubbard.

You're not going to meet new people to add to your network if you don't talk to them. To reinforce Rick Frishman's wise words: "You might be standing in line next to your future husband or the person who will give you your next job. Call it luck, call it fate, but you can't call it anything if you don't open your mouth and say hello."

At the same time, starting a conversation with a stranger can be daunting. However, it can be less intimidating if you approach starting a conversation in a relaxed way, with the understanding that sometimes you will get a response, but if you don't, there are always new connections to make further down the road. Think of the process as one of:

1) Making a *connection* that leads to

2) A *conversation*, and then hopefully

3) A *collaboration*.

FIRST MAKE THE CONNECTION

The wonderful thing about first making a connection is that it gives you an opportunity to test the waters. Start off casually. You never need to start a conversation by introducing yourself, or your job title, to the other person. That can come later. Start a conversation by making a comment about your surroundings, the level of noise, or the décor. You may even compliment the other person on what they are wearing, and ask them where they got it. Greatly original… NO! But do these simple comments work as conversation openers? Why, YES!

Look around you for ideas. Check out the room or meeting hall: there must be something there that can trigger a conversation with the stranger standing next to you. Is there something interesting about the room, or is there an attractive painting on the wall?

If you're in a place where there is nothing concrete to talk about, you can always use the food or drinks as a starting point. But avoid a comment that can only elicit a yes or no response. That means avoiding "Isn't the food good?" as an opener. Rather, try something like, "this fish reminds me of trips I used to make to the shore." This kind of comment will hopefully prompt the other person to ask you questions in return. Open-ended questions allow people to elaborate and this creates conversation. You are drawing the person out and making them become part of a conversation.

CONVERSATIONAL OPENERS IN ACTION

I once had an entire conversation with someone walking the bridge into CNN Center about how badly equipped Atlanta residents are for cold weather. My brief comment to Jill about not having the right attire...THE CONNECTION... started an entire CONVERSATION. We then agreed to meet for coffee downstairs at CNN Center sometime, and exchanged cards.

The next time it was really cold I remembered our conversation and called Jill, asking her if she would like to meet for coffee. That was the start of a long and fruitful COLLABORATION, as Jill turned out to be a video editor, who has since edited many of my tapes for presentations. I have now become an endless source of freelance work for Jill, and I have an experienced editor in my Rolodex. And this all started with a comment about the weather!

Also, very helpful in making conversation is to remember that *everyone* has three things in common… a PAST, a PRESENT and a FUTURE. You can base an entire conversation with a person by keeping this in mind.

When I had to interview a champion middleweight boxer, on the radio, at only a moment's notice, this came in very handy.

There I was live on radio, when my producer said, "Nadia, you have ten seconds to air." What do you ask when you've done no research whatsoever and are not a boxing fan? Well, first he has a PAST: "When did you first know you wanted to be a boxer? When was your first win? Who inspired your boxing career?"

And he has a PRESENT: "Now, what fight are you currently training for? What is a day in your life like in this phase of your career?"

Finally, he has a FUTURE: "Tell me, what does the future hold for you? Who would you like to fight that you haven't as yet? At what age will you think enough is enough?"

The interview went very well, and my producers were impressed. With these three simple hooks in mind, past, present and future, an entire conversation can flow.

Not everyone is a middleweight boxing champion, but most people will respond if you ask them where they were born or moved from, what their current challenges and experiences are, where their children go to school, and what their goals and aims are.

Remember, to start a conversation, you DO NOT need to immediately introduce yourself. You can simply start with a comment or an observation. This takes the pressure of rejection off. The other person will either respond to your comment, or if they don't, nothing is lost. It's like saying "Hi" to a stranger you pass on the street. If they respond, it's fine and if they don't, it's no big deal. But a casual comment can sometimes lead to a friendship and/or a networking relationship.

CONTINUING THE CONVERSATION

Once you have launched into a conversation that will hopefully lead to a collaboration, there are some basic strategies you can use to keep the conversation going. To start with, it is important that you avoid asking too many questions. The person you are talking with should not feel as if he or she is being interviewed. Quickly asking a lot of questions will only make the other person feel uncomfortable and leave them looking for a way out of the conversation before it has really begun.

Humor is always helpful. You don't have to be a stand-up comedian, but telling a funny story can help break the ice. You'd be surprised how sharing something humorous that happened to you will get others to open up. Everyone loves to laugh and laughing makes people feel comfortable. This is a surefire way to lighten up the tension and get people talking.

Make the other person comfortable by giving them the opportunity to choose a topic. Also, be careful not to invade their personal space. Stand far enough away to give them breathing room, but close enough to be able to clearly hear them.

Pay attention to the messages you're sending out with your body. Are you frowning at the room in general with folded arms? Are you standing rigidly with a pasted-on smile, looking like you're frozen to the spot? If so, you're sending out very clear signals which warn people to steer clear of you because you're just not interested in engaging with them.

Do your Homework

If you're not sure about the interests of the people you're about to meet, it's a good idea to check on the nightly news before you head off to the party. General knowledge and a working understanding of breaking news issues provide great conversation starters when all else fails. If you haven't had time to stay up to date on current affairs, some knowledge of the latest celebrity gossip can also help break the ice.

If you're going to a professional function which represents a networking opportunity, it would be a good idea to do some research beforehand. Prepare some conversation starters that convey the impression that you are knowledgeable about their field of interest.

If you are prepared to throw out plenty of conversational opening lines and have trained yourself to ask open-ended and appropriate questions, you will quickly find that the art of conversation is much easier than you would have ever imagined.

Chapter 5

Strengthening Your Networking Confidence

Nothing is so contagious as enthusiasm; it moves stones, it charms brutes. Enthusiasm is the genius of sincerity, and truth accomplishes no victories without it.

— Edward Bulwer-Lytton,
British politician, poet and novelist.

There is no doubt that you are much more effective, have a greater chance of attracting people to you, and generating the kind of response you want to get if you exude confidence. Positive energy attracts and negative energy repels. This is particularly true in networking.

First, you have to believe in yourself. Then you are in a position to communicate your sense of confidence to the other person so that they believe what you have is valuable. In this way, you are able to radiate a "life is good to me, would you like to know my secret?" attitude that will work wonders by attracting rather than alienating people.

Are there people in your life that you cannot bear to be around because they have that "negative persona?" Be aware of the level of energy you are exuding. You may not even be conscious of moments when you are in a negative state, nor even be aware that other people can see it, and that you are sabotaging yourself.

I learned this the hard way. When I first left South Africa, I thought it was important for every single person I met to know how traumatic it was to emigrate. I thought everybody I met should know what terrible pain I was in. So I'm meeting somebody and I'm telling her about the agony of leaving, and all the great things that I have left behind.

Susan looks at me, and I will never forget what she said. "Nadia, I think you've a very nice person, and I think you've very talented, but I can't work with you."

"But why?" I asked, quite stunned.

Susan said, "Because you're in too much pain."

At the time I thought, What an unkind person. But you know what? She wasn't my best friend. I hadn't developed a relationship with Susan where she

would care. And basically, she didn't want to take on all my problems. In retrospect, I understand her position very well.

CREATE A POSITIVE EMOTIONAL MEMORY DISC

One of the best techniques to radiate positive energy and overcome self-doubt is the creation of your own Positive Emotional Memory Disc™. Focusing on past successes and recalling a positive feeling enables your body to automatically relax and respond.

Start reflecting on memorable moments of triumph you have experienced. These memories can be anything from the exhilaration of winning that tough competition, to capturing a scholarship to your dream school, or interviewing successfully to land that perfect job. (Note: an exercise to apply your memorable moments is coming up.)

Once you have your own original catalog of positive memories, it is vital that you constantly "refresh" your disc with new positive experiences so that your memories are immediately accessible. It should become an essential part of your thought process and eventually quite effortless.

"File" these memories as you would file your music on an iPod. "Carry" them with you as your reservoir of confidence tools to draw on when you need them. The goal is to relive these experiences in all their glorious detail and commit them to memory where they can be pulled up as easily as your next appointment on your Blackberry.

What Experience Is On Nadia Bilchik's Positive Emotional Memory Disc™?

On occasions when I need to evoke wonderful feelings of enthusiasm and confidence, I reflect on hosting the Women In Film awards with Alfre Woodward. I can clearly see the red dress I was wearing, and I can recapture the feeling of joy as she complimented me on a job well done. I can still see the audience, hear the applause, and taste the champagne that was served.

Use Your Positive Memories To Overcome The Negative

You will find that your Positive Emotional Memories will be a big help when you need to overcome the negatives, as in this experience of mine:

I clearly remember accessing my Positive Emotional Memory Disc when I was auditioning at Georgia Public Television for a show called Homes For Better Living. An hour before the allotted time, I received a phone call from a superior who berated me for a perceived error and did not give me any chance at all to explain myself. I had only been in the United States for a few months, and I was devastated and convinced that my career had been ruined. This was not true of course, but I didn't know it at the time.

So after collapsing into tears, I braced myself for the audition. As I was driving downtown, I remembered to access my disc, my reservoir of positive emotional memories. Simply by recalling a moment of triumph (the Women In Film experience) I was able to defuse the humiliation and feel less traumatized.

As soon as I arrived at GPTV, I was called into the room and asked by the producer to recall the script. In my emotional state, I had overlooked even glancing at it, and told the producer that I would rather improvise.

I looked straight into the camera, and gave a wonderful description of a silver and white Christmas. It worked, I got the job, and the following week, the pilot of Homes For Better Living aired.

I had a choice when I went into that audition. I could have told them my sad tale of woe, which may have gotten me their sympathy, but definitely not the job. The decision I made, to walk in with confidence and exude positive energy, is what made me successful.

Exercise: *Burn Your Own "Positive Emotional Memory" Disc*

Take 10 - 15 minutes to write down at least three positive, personal experiences that validate, enforce and remind you of your ability. These experiences should evoke feelings of confidence and triumph.

After you have written down these experiences, describe how they made you feel at the time.

Write down at least three positive attributes that you feel these memories reflect.

Now, imagine three situations in which it would be helpful to access your P.E.M. disc, and write them down.

In a book called *Mind Power*, John Kehoe wrote that while most people believe they are only as good as their last experience, that is just not true. We are a combination of all of our successes. Just because you've having a bad day, all that past success doesn't go away.

Sometimes you need help with that positive vibration and sometimes it's automatically there. And if it's taking a day off, what could you do?

One very effective "mind trick" is to think about how famous Olympic champions prepare for the dive of a lifetime. How do they do it? It's time to do the dive. To psyche themselves up, in their head they "play a video" of the perfect dive. Then they stand up on the diving board and *visualize* themselves performing this perfect dive, as they've done before in other competitions. Then they execute the perfect dive.

Sometimes you just need to remind yourself how successful you've been, and it's particularly helpful on days when you're going through a confidence low.

POSITIVE SELF-TALK

According to Honore de Belzac, "Nothing is a greater impediment to getting on well with other people than being ill at ease with yourself." Our inner dialogue—what we communicate to ourselves—has a huge impact on the way we project ourselves in our outer world. So often it is our unconscious negativity that sabotages us. While this is probably not news to you, we all have to be reminded to be conscious of all the negative messages we send ourselves. If we change our thinking, we can learn to avoid the mire of self-destruction.

Ask yourself the following questions:

- Am I clear on my intent?

- Am I conscious of what it is exactly that I want to say?

- Am I giving myself a positive outcome?

- Am I excited about my content?

All too often we allow our state of mind to reflect in our attitude. We forget that sometimes all we need to do is act UP, even when we are feeling DOWN. That little strategy alone can get you over most hurdles that may come your way.

Chapter 6
Building Rapport &
Relationships

When dealing with people, remember that you are not dealing with creatures of logic but creatures of emotion.

— Dale Carnegie

As the Atlanta-based sales and presentation guru, Ken Futch, so wisely points out: "We all have a primary style of operating. While it is important to know our own, the power comes in understanding how to relate to other personality styles."

This is so true. We obviously resonate and connect more with some people than others. Each and every one of us relates to people differently. Some of us are very open and share personal details quickly. Others are more reserved and would never think of discussing our personal lives on first meeting. There are those people who leave a meeting having noticed the tension that existed between two colleagues, and there are those so focused on the task at hand that this went by unnoticed.

What are you?

- A leader or a follower?

- Reserved, or open?

- Introverted or extroverted?

- People focused, or task-oriented?

- Rational or intuitive?

- A thinker or a feeler?

- Sociable or a "loner?"

- Empathetic and aware of other people's emotional reactions?

- Emotionally "tone deaf" and unable to sense how other people are feeling?

Dr. Tony Alessandro, who is a professor of marketing, as well as a highly respected motivational and marketing expert, is one of many observers who have realized that one of the most important keys to building successful relationships is developing an awareness of other people's relating styles. As he notes: "It is only by understanding the nuances through which other individuals see the world that we can begin to relate to them in a meaningful way. When you treat people the way you want to be treated, you create relationship tension;

when you treat people the way they want to be treated, you build rapport."

To relate to people more successfully, it is important to learn how to read their verbal, vocal (voice inflections), and visual signals, and then adapt your behavior to accommodate their behavioral style. Some individuals find it easy to converse with strangers and will quickly share relatively personal information. Others are more reserved and may need time to feel comfortable in a new social situation before opening up. While the more open person would probably enjoy a personal interaction that is warm, lively and open, the more reserved individual is likely to shut down and "head for the hills" if approached too quickly.

Individuals with different personality characteristics also prefer different kinds of communication styles. For example, people who have strong leadership qualities usually appreciate direct, results-oriented communication. A creative type, on the other hand, might respond well to communication that refers to his or her field of interest. This kind of individual may not be interested in details, but will appreciate being given time to plan and accomplish his or her own work.

Meanwhile, an introverted, detail-oriented individual is not likely to respond well to overenthusiastic behavior that he or she feels is impinging on his or her personal space. This kind of personality will probably prefer to be given as many details as possible, and appreciates time to gather information and decide on solutions.

Some people value interpersonal relationships, while others are more comfortable as "loners." While a person who is invested in interpersonal relationships may value expressions of appreciation and support, a "loner" may feel uncomfortable in that kind of situation, and prefer a certain distance. It is important to be sensitive to these kinds of individuals' needs for interpersonal validation.

Expert Networking is essentially a form of marketing yourself. And, knowing your personality type, as well as recognizing others', will give you a distinct advantage.

Allesandro has identified four basic business personalities:

- Directors
- Socializers
- Relaters, and
- Thinkers.

The *Director*, for example, is results-oriented, decisive and direct, while the *Thinker* is careful, detailed and reserved.

The *Relater* is likely to be friendly and avoid conflict, while the *Socializer* is enthusiastic and creative.

The *Director* is likely to say things like, "I want it now!" and the *Socializer* is more likely to say something like, "I've got a great idea!"

Dr. Allesandro suggests using a range of strategies to communicate effectively with people of different personalities.

For the *Director*, it is important to focus on results and give direct answers.

The *Thinker* prefers to be given as many details as possible, and appreciates time to gather information and decide on solutions.

The *Socializer* is not a detail person, and appreciates freedom to plan and accomplish his or her work.

And the *Relater* values expressions of appreciation and support.

Expert Networkers consciously adjust their language to adapt to those with whom they are working, and even plan the best way to start a conversation. While you are working on this skill, remember that the essence of good conversation is to communicate to the other person that you truly understand where they are coming from. Remember, people don't care what you know until they know that you care.

Exercise: *Interacting With Other Business Personalities*

Write down what you think your personality or style is.

Think about a person outside of work with whom you have a relationship. Based on his or her personality traits, explain how you have or have not gotten along with the person.

Think about an important person at work that you get along with. What kind of business personality do they have?

Try to identify some of the ways you communicate and work with this person. Do you think you have adapted your relating style to this person?

Identify a person in your work environment who you have trouble relating to. What kind of business personality does this person have?

Based on what you now know about the four business personalities, what could you do differently with the people you have identified to create more harmony?

To accelerate your communication skills, redo this exercise with people in mind who exemplify each of the four business personality types.

MY EXAMPLE OF RELATING TO ANOTHER STYLE

I am an extrovert, and a person Dr. Allesandro would call a *Socializer*. If I only networked or connected with people who I felt an instant rapport with, I would be tremendously limited.

When I first met Nancy Neill, the President of Atlanta Communications Group, she was very reserved. If I did not have the knowledge that her reservation was part of her PERSONALITY STYLE, I would have mistaken it for being standoffish and may not have persevered with our conversation.

But I was able to identify that Nancy was the kind of person who is initially guarded, a THINKER. My realization that she operates differently than the way I do, meant that I needed to take the interaction more slowly than I naturally would. I knew that Nancy needed to assess the situation, whereas I was impulsive. As a result of my patience and understanding of her different operating style, we have become great friends and I have had the pleasure of working with her many times.

In sum, the more you are aware of another person's business personality, and how it corresponds to yours, the easier networking becomes.

CHAPTER 7

THE F.I.R.E. APPROACH TO NETWORKING

There is nothing we like to see so much as the gleam of pleasure in a person's eye when he feels that we have sympathized with him, understood him, interested ourselves in his welfare. At these moments something fine and spiritual passes between two friends. These moments are the moments worth living.

— Don Marquis

Now that we have covered the basics, it's time to put it all together. Networking does not require you to be pushy. That's a myth. Besides, just making a connection is not enough. When we network, we need to become a relationship builder. For many people, this is much easier said than done. So to give you some guidelines, I have developed the F.I.R.E. approach to networking, which is defined as follows:

Feel good about yourself.

Interest: show genuine interest in the person you are relating to.

Relax yourself (which will relax the other person as well).

Engage the other person with your energy and enthusiasm.

Now, to break it down for you:

F - As mentioned in Chapter Two, you have to feel good about yourself, and by this stage, if you participated in the exercises, you've developed the kinds of self-talk strategies and positive memories that can do the trick. Remember, nothing is a greater impediment to getting on well with other people than being ill at ease with yourself. As one anonymous sage pointed out: "Cheerfulness is contagious, but don't wait to catch it from others, be a carrier."

However, if you still do not have a strong sense of confidence in yourself at this point in the book, please go back and review Chapter Two and Chapter Five.

I - It is essential that you show genuine interest in the person you are relating to.

As Dale Carnegie said, "You can make more friends being interested in other people than in two years getting them interested in you." He also said, "People who talk about others are gossips, people who talk about themselves are bores, and people who talk about *you* are brilliant conversationalists!"

People want to be valued. On a far more serious note, Carnegie contended that individuals who do not take an interest in others have "the greatest difficulties in life and provide the greatest injury to others." He added that it is from those kinds of self-centered people that "all human failures spring!"

We also need to show interest in a way that is most appealing to the type of person we are relating to. There are many names for this ability. Some call it empathy, some call it reading people well, and others call it Emotional Intelligence. Very simply put, it is the ability to see the world through another person's eyes. So how does one embark on a conversation with anyone at anytime, and anyplace?

Interest is not only shown by what you say, but is enhanced by your eye contact and body language. Of course, you do not want to stare soulfully into the eyes of a stranger, and you definitely want to respect their personal space. But you can show interest in more subtle ways by angling your shoulders slightly toward the person, and definitely by giving them your full attention. This means not scanning the room for other potentially interesting people while you are engaged in this encounter.

ACTIVE LISTENING

To be an effective communicator, you must be tuned in to the other person's feelings. You can do this through *active listening.* Active listening encourages communication and puts other people at ease. Active listening also clarifies what is being said.

STEPS TO BEING AN ACTIVE LISTENER

- Look the other person directly in the eyes when they talk to you, and *maintain* eye contact.

- Be conscious about not letting your mind wander. If you realize you have been thinking about the day's to-do list, catch yourself and bring your focus back.

- Avoid looking at things that could distract your attention (such as other people or a TV in the room).

- Be aware of body language, both yours and the other person's. (For example, do not look at your watch or shift around in your chair.)

- Focus on what the other person is saying, rather than on what your response will be.

- Smile slightly, but do not laugh loudly. (This way, you won't look like you're trying too hard to please.)

- Let the other person have his or her moment. (Do not try to one-up them with your better joke, or worse experience.)

- Listen closely and do not interrupt the other person, except to ask clarifying or qualifying questions like "How did it make you feel?"

- Reflect back to the other person by rephrasing what they have said. (This will make it clear that you have understood their message.)

- Pay specific and sincere compliments.

Genuine interest is a powerful thing. We don't always remember what someone says, but we remember the way they made us feel about ourselves. Sometimes with friends I make a point of listening and asking questions that help me understand more fully what they are saying. It is always tempting to try to bring the conversation back to your own concerns, and it takes discipline and self awareness to give your full attention to the other individual. The benefit of this is they will feel that you are really listening to them.

R - You need to be as relaxed as possible in all interactions. If you're not relaxed, others will sense your tension and become uncomfortable, perhaps even recoil. There are few things more uncomfortable than the feeling that a person *wants* something from you. There is a feeling of desperation about it. You want someone to be comfortable and confident that this is a long-term investment in a relationship that has the potential to grow and evolve.

I have found that an easy-going approach eliminates a great deal of anxiety in the networking process. As a reminder, you don't need to go up to a person and immediately introduce yourself along with your occupation. Rather, start a relaxed conversation based on an observation of something happening in the immediate vicinity. If the person is responsive to you and a rapport develops, then introduce yourself and talk about what you do for a living. That approach takes a lot of the pressure off. Just forget about the titles and talk. And remember, as Alvin Toffler said: "The less you need something, the more power you have."

E - Engage the other person with a high level of energy and enthusiasm. Nothing sells like enthusiasm and by radiating positive energy you are far more likely to attract the kind of person that you would like to network with. As Ralph Waldo Emerson wrote, "Vigor is contagious, and whatever makes us think or feel strongly, adds to our power and enlarges our field of action." So, this is not the time to let people know that you can't stand your current job and are actively looking for a new one. Similarly, don't share the fact that you dislike your co-workers, or the neighborhood you live in. Rather, focus on the positives, and communicate the kind of positive energy that will attract people to you.

Chapter 8
Casual or Incidental Networking

Every day fishing day, but not every day catch fish.

— Bahamian proverb

We have defined the true nature of networking and analyzed the factors that may personally stop us from taking full advantage of networking opportunities. We have discussed strategies for projecting a sense of confidence, developing rapport, and relating to different personality types.

Now we will look at situations where you can put this knowledge into practice. The general rule of all of this is: *network most when you need it least*. Or, as Harvey Mackay, author of *Swim With the Sharks Without Being Eaten Alive* says, "Dig your well before you're thirsty."

One common scenario is the casual, incidental networking opportunity. These are moments such as at your child's soccer game, the hairdresser, or the company cafeteria, when a brief connection develops into a conversation. It is those kinds of moments that can sometimes evolve into a collaboration, because you never know when or how you might meet someone whose life can impact yours.

The question at hand is: "How does one light the F.I.R.E., or build rapport in a casual, or incidental networking environment?"

How many times have you just met someone casually while standing in line, or at a restaurant, watching a school soccer game, or at the company cafeteria? How often has this type of brief connection developed into a conversation? How often still has this evolved into a collaboration?

Take a moment to think of the many opportunities you have every day to mingle, meet and converse with someone new. For me, a simple stroll on the bridge from the parking lot to the CNN building has resulted in many conversations, which have led to a second meeting, and finally turned into a networking collaboration.

It was because of such a chance encounter that I met CNN Promo Producer David Tooch. One day, a gentleman happened to be walking a few feet in front of me and I simply commented on his rather unusual backpack, which had Hebrew lettering on it. As we neared the end of the bridge leading into the CNN building, I asked him which department he was with. He said, "Promos," and that gave me the opportunity to ask if they ever needed voice talent. Enthusiastically, he said, "We certainly do," and gave me his card. I now do regular voice-overs for the CNN International Promo Department. And there's more. It was during one of my voice-over sessions that I learned about the CNN Guest Bookings Department and was encouraged to apply because of my networking and communications skills. Now, as a freelance Editorial Guest Producer, I identify and book experts around the world to appear on CNN International.

Anther reason casual, incidental meetings can be invaluable is because...

You never know: the person you meet may KNOW the person you need to meet.

This happened to me when I first arrived in Atlanta: I was sitting in a packed downtown restaurant. The tables were so close together that my chair was literally touching the next table. It was my comment about this to the friendly lady whose chair abutted mine that started us chatting. She heard my accent and asked where I was from, thus launching a lively conversation about how cosmopolitan Atlanta was becoming.

Only later did we exchange names and cards. Ney Lawson (by now I had found out her name) and I arranged to have lunch at the same restaurant a few weeks later. We realized after our initial connection that we both had a lot in common. For one thing, she was an art collector; and my husband and I have an extensive collection of South African art. Ney was an instant hit with our children and soon became what I now refer to as our "Fairy Godmother."

It was a year or so later when I was having a conversation with executives at Coca-Cola, that my relationship with Ney could be defined as a networking one. Coke was looking for a speaker for their mentor program. The brief was, "Preferably female, preferably someone very high profile..." And, "someone like Carol Mosley-Braun" was the description. Within twenty minutes I had Carol Mosley-Braun herself booked as their next speaker. You see, Carol and Ney are long-time friends, and had been in touch throughout Carol's career as a lawyer, and then Ambassador to New Zealand. Because of my relationship with Ney, I had the privilege of accessing her vast network, and Carol was amongst them.

But, when I met Ney, did I think, "This is a good contact?" No. I thought, "This is a nice person."

THE IMPORTANCE OF DEVELOPING RAPPORT

I try and have my "What can I do for you?" antenna switched on whenever I have chance encounters. But given their brief nature, it is not always easy. That is why you must *first* develop rapport. You build a connection that says, "This seems like a person who would be nice to get to know better." *Think about the endless people you have met that seem interesting, but subsequently faded out of your life because neither of you followed up and developed a "What can we do for each other?" relationship.* When people fade out of your life you never get the benefit of having real access to each other's network.

I recently found myself at a dinner party sitting next to the CEO of a major electronics company. He was someone who had the potential to be a good contact for my business. I knew nothing about him, but based on the PAST, PRESENT and FUTURE frame, I asked him, (PAST) "Did you always know what you wanted to do?" And, "When did you land your first deal?" (PRESENT) "What are your current challenges? And your frustrations?" (FUTURE) "Do you have any exciting new projects planned?" With that, an entire conversation ensued, and later I was able to arrange a meeting and discuss the various programs I offer. This resulted in several coaching sessions for his management team as well as a keynote address at his annual board meeting. All this transpired because

I was mentally prepared to engage him (or anyone else for that matter) in a comfortable conversation.

As you can see, these principles can be applied to any conversation as long as you apply the F.I.R.E. rule. First *feel good* about yourself, and then show genuine *interest*. Be *relaxed* in your approach and *engage* them with your enthusiasm.

Sample Questions Based on the Framework of Past, Present and Future

PAST:

- Where are you from, originally?

- What school did you go to?

- How long have you been here?

PRESENT:

- What do you do for fun? (interests? hobbies?)

- What do you enjoy about your job?

- Where do you live?

- How do you like your neighborhood?

FUTURE:

- What's next for you?

- Do you expect to live in your town for the rest of your life?

AT A MIXER, OR FORMAL NETWORKING EVENT:

- How long have you been with the company?

- Where have you worked before?

- What do you do for the company?

- What projects are you currently working on?

- Are you planning to stay in this job?

- Where do you see yourself in five years' time?

I never go up to somebody and formally introduce myself, then start talking. I keep it as casual and nonchalant as possible. And I've almost always found that most people are ready to have a little chat.

PLACES TO STRIKE UP A CONVERSATION

- Your child's soccer field (other parents)

- Grocery store (waiting in line)

- Cafeteria (sit with a different group)

- Parking garage (waiting for the valet)

- Airport / Airplanes (that person sitting next to you)

- Company picnic (during a softball game)

- Starbucks (their first name is written on their cup)

- City park (while walking your dog)

- Bookstore (while browsing)

- Art Gallery (in line for the free wine)

- Library (at a special event)

- Sporting events (the seats N, W, S, and E of you)

- Volunteer events (a local neighborhood clean-up, or tree planting)

Starter Phrases

- "I am always amazed that they have so little staff at peak hour!"

- "I can't imagine my life before Starbucks."

- "This is the first flight that I've been on this month that hasn't been delayed."

- "Do you think it could get any colder/hotter in here?"

- "I love shopping here; this market always has the freshest-looking produce!"

- "I see you're getting [BOOK TITLE], have you read any of his/her other books?"

- "I'm really impressed with this gallery's new artist; the way he/she mixes colors is almost magical."

- "Great service here—I get the feeling the valets are secretly Olympic sprinters."

- "This is my favorite dog-walking park; what breed is yours?"

TOPICS THAT ARE EASY TO SAY SOMETHING NONCHALANT ABOUT

- The weather

- The parking situation

- Fashion ("Where did you get those great looking shoes?" "Who cuts your hair?)

- School ("What school do your children go to?")

- Natural disasters in the news

- Traffic ("Do you think they're ever going to add another lane?")

- Commuting ("I have a long commute to work every day, how about you?")

- The service (at a store or restaurant)

- The décor ("Beautiful flowers!" "Aren't these creative table settings?")

- Local happenings in your town

TOPICS TO BE CAREFUL WITH:

Be wary of making comments on topics that can be polarizing, like politics, religion, or American foreign policy. People can have very strong views on these kinds of topics, and you may find yourself in a heated discussion with an individual you do not know well.

On the other hand, if the other person shares their opinions *first*, and your views are similar, then these subjects can be optimal for building rapport.

IT'S YOUR PARTY...

Another extremely useful networking technique in both casual and formal networking environments such as a cocktail party, is to play the role of host or hostess. I call this the attitude of, "It's my party, and I will introduce myself to others who I want to." Try it. You will be surprised at how effective this can be. For example, the next time you are at a social event, rather than waiting to be introduced, make the introductions yourself. If you observe two strangers standing awkwardly next to each other, engage them and make introductions ("Hello, have you two met?" Or, "Oh, do you two know each other?"), as if they were guests at your party. In this way, you'll learn their names, and their gratitude for helping to break the ice.

Remember, in both casual and incidental networking opportunities, your life does not depend on it. You do not need to formally introduce yourself. You can make a relaxed comment like, "Can you believe how many tables they fit in here?" Or, "Is it always such a long line?" Or, on a positive note, "Can you believe how good the service is here?" The point is, by making a casual comment, you can initiate the conversation and then determine if you want to introduce yourself by name and continue the discussion.

In the same way that champions in sports practice visualizations, you can do something similar. This will help you approach your next chance encounter with confidence, rather than fear. By now, you should be able to answer the following questions in the affirmative:

- "Am I at ease with making conversation and with my general social skills?"

- "Am I taking advantage of every opportunity to meet someone new?"

- "Do I approach situations thinking, 'I never know who I might meet?'"

As Henry David Thoreau wrote, "If one advances with confidence and positive energy in the direction of ones dreams and endeavors to live the life which he has imagined, he will meet with success unexpected in common hours."

RECOGNIZING WHEN NETWORKING IS NOT WORTH THE EFFORT.

In his seminal book, *Emotional Intelligence*, Daniel Goleman makes the point that personal qualities like self-discipline, self-awareness and empathy are as vital to success as a high I.Q. Indeed, one of the most important skills an *Expert Networker* can develop is finesse—or being able to "read" people's reactions. The skill here is recognizing whether or not your networking "target" is interested in the relationship or not.

For example, notice their body language:

- Is the person facing you, or looking away?

- Is he or she responding to or blocking the conversation?

- If it is two or more people, are they talking around you?

EXIT STRATEGIES

If somebody is not responding to your efforts to initiate conversation, or to continue a conversation, you'll probably want to remove yourself from this uncomfortable situation. Don't worry about hurting their feelings. If someone clearly does not want to have a conversation with you, don't torture yourself, or them. Move on. But here are some exit lines to make it a little easier:

- "I'm going to go and get a drink, would you like me to get you anything?" (Note: if they say "no," just say, "Nice meeting you!" and make your exit.)

- "It was really nice to meet you, let me give you a card."

- "Please excuse me, there is Jack Smith, and I really need to talk to him."

- "Lovely to speak to you, enjoy the evening."

THE "BOOKMARK" STRATEGY

What if you're in the middle of a conversation, you see someone else you want to meet, but still want to develop the relationship with the person you are talking to? Say something like...

- "I need to talk to Jane over there before she leaves, but I really want to finish what we were talking about."

- "That was really interesting information that you shared with me. Please give me your card, so that I can follow up with you soon."

- "A colleague of mine has a lot of expertise in your field, and I know you will enjoy meeting each other. Let's all plan to get together."

ENTRANCE STRATEGIES

Sometimes you will walk into a room when you're on your own and everyone seems to be engaged in conversations with each other. There is apparently no host for the event and no one is making introductions. How do you enter into a conversation already in progress between two or more people? First off, keep in mind that people will react to the energy that you exude. This is where the "It's my party" attitude will come in handy. People love confidence and if you approach any conversation-in-progress like you are very comfortable in your shoes, they will instantly warm to you. Again, don't introduce yourself right off the bat. Make a comment that they can respond to, such as…

- "Man, the traffic was bad coming from the north, how was it for you?"

- "Have the formalities started yet?"

- "Have you tried the buffet yet, and is there anything you recommend?"

- "I'm going to find the bar. Can I get a drink for anyone?"

Exercise: *Make Your Own Inventory*

Take a few minutes and make a mental inventory of your everyday activities. I'm sure you'll realize that your daily life is a cornucopia of casual or incidental networking opportunities. Go over the list of possible venues that come to mind, and write down those that you think could provide opportunities for you as you go about your day. (And make sure to take advantage of them in the near future.)

Remember that the best networking opportunities happen when you are not tense, anxious or in need. If you need to build up your confidence, you can even practice these skills in situations where you have nothing at stake—like at a neighborhood party. At the very least, you could make a new friend. And you never know what kinds of networking rewards you may get.

As a final reminder, if you keep at the forefront of your mind that everyone has a PAST, a PRESENT and a FUTURE, you will never run out of topics for a conversation.

CHAPTER 9
FORMAL TARGETED NETWORKING

There are no shortcuts to any place worth going.
— Beverly Sills

How do you develop relationships and alliances without being labeled as pushy? How do you go about strategically getting into a situation where you have a better chance of arranging that meeting or targeting that opportunity?

Here is what is called targeted networking for a particular purpose: to gain access to the right people, the right opportunity, and the right connections in your industry.

The first thing you have to do is become involved; show up, and bring all you have to the table. The next requirement is to have something of value to bring to the network. "It is vital," writes networking and marketing expert Rick Frishman, "that you obtain and maintain expert knowledge in a particular area."

Bring it all to the Table

To "become involved, show up and bring all you have to the table" means picking a few important places to spend your time and really becoming invested, so others can see your commitment and want to invest in you. Being involved in a forum or a group is one of the best ways, preferably as an active board member, so that people associate you with this organization, and get to know you.

Use networking events productively. Pick a few important places to spend your time and really become involved so others can see and admire your commitment. *Expert Networkers* pick one or two networking groups related to their profession or hobbies, and start attending these events. To meet people, you could find the event's organizer and ask to be introduced to a few key people.

Formal Networking Venues

The key in networking on this level is access. And the way to access is to comfortably find people through your common interests. To follow are some venues you will find in most communities:

- Mentoring programs

- Annual picnics

- Forums in your company. (For example, Coca-Cola has the Executive Assistants Forum.)

- Boy Scouts / Girl Scouts / Brownies / Big Brothers / Big Sisters

- Volunteer Programs

- Your children's activities (e.g., volunteer to get involved in their sports activities in your children's school, and if you don't have children, volunteer anyway! I know colleagues who have made their best business contacts from friends they made on class trips, or helping to run a school fundraiser.)

- Booster Clubs (hearken back to your college days and get involved with the clubs that are established around your alma mater.)

- Rotary. (Many *Expert Networkers* recommend joining Rotary because a lot of very influential, powerful people often belong. Rotary events give you the opportunity to meet others on an equal level. Similarly, a group like Women in Technology is useful, even if you are not actually working in technology.)

- Wine tasting associations

- Houses of worship (church, synagogue, mosque, temple)

Be discriminating! You don't need to belong to 100 different organizations. Rather, get involved and well known in one or two carefully chosen organizations. A very good strategy would be to join one work and one community-related organization, so that you are raising your profile within your company, but also ensuring access to outside connections.

Venues that relate to your professional interests are particularly valuable. For example, a Georgia-based journalist could go to Atlanta Press Club events. A speaker could get involved with The National Speaker's Association. An accountant might join the American Institute of Certified Public Accountants. And an executive in the hospitality industry would consider the Food and Beverage Association. These kinds of affiliations will help to increase your visibility within that organization, and enable you to become greater than the sum of your individual parts. These affiliations can give you the opportunity to leverage the skills you have outside your job.

You should also consider getting involved in programs within your company. As previously mentioned, Coca-Cola has the Executive Assistants Forum, and Turner Broadcasting has affinity programs, like "Turner Women Today." Company Forums are an excellent way of raising your profile, particularly if you are active on the board, thus giving you access to people in the company you would not otherwise have.

Taking the Forum Route out of a Dead End Job

Bonnie W's Story: *I had been with my company for over 15 years, managing to hang on through two horrible re-organizations the first part of the 2000's. I had a horrible attitude, and hated my job, although I was happy to have one. But I had lost my passion.*

Then I was approached by a friend, who asked if I would be interested in working with a team developing a brand optimization for the Women's Forum. I joined the Forum and became an active member. I met several nice people, enjoyed the work and learned a great deal in the process. My attitude improved.

Then one day, during one of our committee meetings, I met Jane. I had no idea who she was, but was extremely impressed with her. After the meeting, I had some follow-up to forward and looked her up. To my great surprise, she had a position open reporting to her, and it appeared to be the kind of position I was looking for. She is the director of global marketing, supporting some people I worked with in the past. I made a few phone calls to those old friends and then called her directly. Next thing I knew, I had an interview lined up. I used my networking skills to meet with several old bosses and friends for coaching. They were all very excited

---

about my opportunity and helped me immensely. I learned as much as I could in a very short amount of time about the Global Customer Development team, the business model and their customers. I've been on the team for more than six months and just love it. I learn something new every day. I'm fully engaged. My passion has returned. And, I always look forward to meeting new people.

Keep in mind that formal, targeted networking takes time. The connections are made when you interact in the same environment with the same people over and over again. It's seeing the same people at your church, synagogue, or mosque so that you almost feel like friends before you actually meet. It's being on the board of an association and demonstrating your values, your deep concerns or passions, and your savvy.

Nadia Bilchik

Exercise: *Getting Access*

Make an inventory of the forums that are available to you right now.

Identify the ones that will be conducive to meeting certain people in your company, or developing other relationships that could benefit you.

TRUE PROACTIVITY: CREATE YOUR OWN FORUM

If there is nothing in your community for you in terms of associations or organizations, consider being truly proactive and starting your own group on your own terms.

One example of this is Virginia Bradley, who started her own networking group, called GlobalEXEC-women. You can find the website of the organization at *tuesdaywomen.com*. As president of this group of women executives involved in information technology, Bradley has succeeded in elevating her importance, status and value. And, most significantly for our purposes, she has been able to leverage her position to gain incredible access to very important and influential individuals. She has accomplished this because she is able to approach senior executives and power brokers as a representative of a prestigious group, rather than on her own behalf. Accordingly, the important individuals she has approached have been very receptive, because they too are interested in the exposure. They also want the opportunity to speak, explore and show what they have to offer. It is not surprising then, that one of the organization's recent events was held at the offices of the British Consul General in Atlanta!

As you can imagine, when I was once asked to facilitate the group, I was happy to oblige, because it gave me the opportunity to meet those people. Because they were impressed with my performance, I ended up doing one-on-one coaching with some of the participants.

So, do you see how clever Ms. Bradley has been? She's designed an entire formula. She's created for herself the opportunity to have access to a wide variety of people. Now, she can call any one of these people. She's not asking them for a favor, she is inviting them to be part of the forum. She actually makes people feel privileged to be invited to the group. And there are many important people who are beyond the reach of an individual who would be happy to accept an invitation to address a group.

FOOD FOR YOUR NETWORK

Rick Frishman and Jill Lublin developed Board Room Dinners. The invitees are always top people in their respective fields. The host always does a lot of preparation work to make sure there will be great discussions. This includes preparing questions about what the experts are working on, and figuring out how the experts work in order to relate to one another. To keep the process of networking and conversation going, the hosts make sure that many people get the chance to speak. Also, the hosts are responsible for changing the topic if a particular discussion starts to lose steam.

To create your own forum, research the Internet. Find other forums already in operation. Get in touch with the person who started the forum, or one of the members. Then "pick their brain" for information. Find out how their forum operates (attend a meeting if necessary). Then devise your own game plan on your terms.

Exercise: *More on Accessing those Hard-to-Reach People*

Answer the following questions:

- "What forums are available to you now?"

- "How active are you?"

- "Is this sufficient to meet new people on a regular basis?"

- "How high profile are you?"

- "How can you leverage your position?"

Spend 10 minutes brainstorming ideas to get more involved in forums, or to create your own.

NETWORK SHARING (CONNECTING OTHERS)

If you do arrange a meeting with someone you see as instrumental to your career advancement, make sure you frame your interaction in such a way that validates and respects their advice. I am always put off by people who DEMAND access to my network. Networking or sharing your highly valued group of allies is a privilege. It is not a right.

As an example of someone who needed something from me and approached it in the wrong way:

I had an incident recently where somebody called me knowing I work at CNN and basically demanded to spend three days with me at my job. She didn't even ask. What she said was, "Nadia, I'm going to be in Atlanta for three days, and I'm coming to see you because I want to work at CNN." She assumed she had the right because our parents are friends, and it totally irritated me.

Had she asked differently, I would have been happy to help her. As it turned out, I did meet with her, but it was out of obligation because of the relationship between her and my parents. But I did not do any of the extra legwork. Rather than call one of my contacts with her resume, I just directed her to the Turner job website.

An approach that is far more likely to get good results is to let the person you would like to meet know what you are hoping to achieve. Then ask them if they have a recommendation for how you might proceed. I cannot stress enough the power of HOW YOU ASK versus WHAT YOU ASK. It is essential that you consider carefully how you *frame* the request in such a way that invites rather than repels assistance.

Frame your request in a respectful way. The "How do you suggest I proceed?" line is a very good one. Also, remember that people feel good about doing good. But always be sure to acknowledge what they have done for you. Once you have accepted someone's advice, it is essential that you be appreciative and follow up. (This will be discussed in detail in a later chapter.)

Finally, remember that *Expert Networking* is a creative process. It should not be seen as linear. There is no definitive route to getting to where you want to be. Sometimes it means getting to know someone's executive assistant. Sometimes it works when you become active on the board of a forum, committee, or club. And sometimes it simply means that you strike up a conversation in the ATM line.

In summary, an *Expert Networker* will make sure to become involved in a group, society, association or forum. Being high profile in a group always gives you better leverage than you would have as an individual, and it allows you to access many hard-to-reach people.

CHAPTER 10

NETWORKING WITH THE POWER-PLAYERS

Generally speaking, the great achieve their greatness by industry, rather than brilliance.

— Bruce Barton

This is the "who I really need to get to" aspect of networking. As if you didn't know it already, it is indeed a challenge to gain access to certain people, like the higher ups in your company, or the CEO of a particular organization who you would like to approach for work. But be assured, it can be done. Try this three-step approach:

Step 1. Know who it is you need to get to know.

Step 2. Contact other people who may have access.

Step 3. Find an additional forum to meet them.

The first step of this process, knowing who it is you need to meet, is usually obvious. For example:

I wanted to offer my Presentation Skills Program to Delta Technology. I knew that the CEO, Curtis Robb, was the decision maker and the person I needed to meet with. Simply calling the company and arranging a meeting with him was not an option. Firstly, he does not meet with vendors he does not know. Secondly, I would come with no references and my chances of actually securing work were minimal.

With a little research I was able to find out that every year Mr. Robb attends the Women In Technology Annual Ball, as Delta Technology is a key sponsor. I offered my services to the WIT Ball organizers as both a volunteer committee member, and the Master of Ceremonies of the evening. I asked Casie Scott Palmer, one of the organizers of the event, to give Mr. Robb some background on me and then introduce us. As Casie was a member of my network, someone who I had invested time and energy in, she was only too pleased to reciprocate. Near the end of the event, Casie introduced us. Mr. Robb and I had a short conversation, and the next day, with his permission I called his office to arrange a meeting. As a result, I have to date delivered numerous presentations to his organization.

There is also an additional point here in that Casie did the ultimate in *Expert Networking*. That was to arrange for us to meet and then make the introduction. Casie is certainly high on my list of people I want to reciprocate to.

But before you try to reach that important person, first do your homework. Make sure you have a very clear idea what this person's role is in the company. Also, without transgressing the boundaries of privacy, try to find out a little bit more about him or her. One source may be the company's own web site, which often provides biographical details about key personnel. It may also be helpful to research recent news and Internet sources, which may yield valuable information. For example, if you can congratulate this person on a recent accomplishment, it will certainly help to make a very positive first impression.

Rick Frishman recommends carefully crafting your message and approach. One way is to develop a networker's toolkit:

- A fabulous sound bite

- A great description of yourself

- Your product or service (and how it benefits others)

- Business cards

- An address list

- A date book

Most importantly be sure you have the expertise to do the job that you want to get.

The Fabulous Sound Bite

What do I mean by a "fabulous sound bite?" A sound bite is usually defined as a very powerful sentence, or short speech on radio or television. For example, a famous historical sound bite is, "We have nothing to fear, but fear itself," from President Franklin D. Roosevelt's inaugural address.

I'm sure that you can think of many more, but what is most important about these "sound bites" is that they stick in your mind and make you memorable. That is why it is important to strive to develop your own sound bite that will leave a lasting impression on other people. It is a form of personal branding that makes you more likely to be remembered when the search is on for new highly qualified staff members, or expert services.

In developing your own fabulous sound bite, it is important that you communicate very clearly what you do. Think of it as trying to paint a picture in people's minds. Give them an example of what you do, and make it short and very tangible. If it is appropriate, you could name some of the skills that you bring to your area of expertise, and give details of a project that exemplifies the work that you do. And, while it is important not to appear boastful, it is fine to give yourself credit for a job well done. Even better, as Peggy Klaus, the author of *Brag!: The Art of Tooting Your Own Horn Without Blowing It*, advises, you should start developing a repertoire that consists of your moments of greatest success.

For example, Mary, who is a project manager in the personnel department of a large communications company could say: "I manage large scale projects that can cause a lot of headaches. Like coordinating the conversion of 8,000 employee IDs into bar codes. And I got it done in three weeks." Bill, who is in sports marketing could say, "I work in sports marketing. You know those trendy [famous sports franchise] bobble heads? I got them placed in every sporting goods store in the state."

YOUR FABULOUS SOUND BITE

It is important that you know exactly what to say when someone asks you, "WHAT YOU DO?" This is where your sound bite comes in handy. Don't just toss out your job title.

Your 10- to 15-second sound bite should explain who you are, what you do, and why you make a difference. You need to do this in a seamless way, sounding very natural.

You need to be able to say…

A) I AM…

B) MY EXPERTISE IS…

C) WHAT I'VE ACHIEVED IS…

For example, my sound bite is:

A) I AM… a producer and guest booker for CNN.

B) MY EXPERTISE IS… I am a lateral thinker, with tremendous initiative and foresight.

C) WHAT I'VE ACHIEVED IS… the ability to deal with breaking news under very tight time pressures. For example, when the Asian Tsunami hit in December, 2005, I rushed into work, and immediately booked 15 major guests for CNN International.

MAKE IT CONVERSATIONAL

You are probably aware that written and spoken language is very different, and it is very easy to tell when a politician is reading a speech off a teleprompter. Once you have developed your sound bite, it is important to craft it so that it sounds conversational, like the sound bites of Mary and Bill mentioned before. The way to do this is to break your sentences down. You even make some grammar errors, because spoken English often has incomplete sentences.

So, if someone says, *What do you do?* I might say, "I work at CNN in the guest bookings department. Remember Tsunami Sunday? I was on call that day, and booked five guests before I even had my first cup of coffee!"

A Business World Example

Steven Spitz, an entrepreneur, says the following when asked what it is he does:

A) I AM... an investor in companies that I can take an active role in managing.

B) MY EXPERTISE IS... I'm very good at bringing highly creative business solutions to non-creative environments.

   OR: What I like to do is look for unconventional ways to dramatically change paradigms.

C) WHAT I'VE ACHIEVED IS... I got creative with a medical rental supply company, and raised its revenues from $35 million to $42 million within two years.

Exercise: *Create Your Fabulous Sound Bite*

Develop your own Fabulous Sound Bite by completing the following:

- I AM...

- MY EXPERTISE IS...

- WHAT I'VE ACHIEVED IS...

Now, refine and revise. Look to your Positive Emotional Memory Disc for inspiration. Then turn your Sound Bite into conversational form by cutting down the length of your sentences, and even using one or two incomplete sentences. Practice your Sound Bite as necessary until it is second nature to you and it just rolls off your tongue—almost without having to think about it. This will have you amply prepared whenever someone important to you pops the question, "And what do you do?"

Volunteer – Early And Often

Canadian sociology professor, Bonnie Erickson, who studies social networks, says that the key to broadening one's social networks is through *volunteerism*. "When you join a voluntary association, you get to meet people who have something in common with you, and you also get to meet people who aren't exactly like you." Thus it's a great way to meet a wide variety of people. Sometimes it is also a great way to get to the Power Players you want to meet.

Readers of the Society pages of newspapers and celebrity magazines have surely noticed that many of the glittering events featured are fundraisers and benefits for a huge range of causes. I want to let you in on a little secret: while the individuals who take part in these events have many commendable motives for participating, they are also taking advantage of the priceless networking opportunities that these kinds of functions offer.

Indeed, volunteering is one of those activities that offer multiple benefits. You will be contributing to a worthy cause, like beautifying a neighborhood, or raising money to help fight a serious disease. But you will also be enriching yourself, both by adding another dimension to who you are, and gaining access to people in a special way that creates a feeling of camaraderie for everyone involved.

It is much easier to meet people when the focus is not on you, but on a cause you and other individuals are working together to benefit. If you and the senior executive you would like to have access to are both working on a neighborhood cleanup, or helping to put up wallboard for an organization like Habitat for Humanity, the social distance and barriers that usually makes access to this kind of individual difficult will definitely be diminished. You will also have a priceless opportunity to show off both your abilities and commendable personal qualities. And you may be able to leverage your encounter into a more formal networking contact later.

How to Find Volunteering Opportunities

Volunteer opportunities abound within the realms of work, family, neighborhood, city and the broader environment. Most large corporations offer a wide range of volunteering opportunities, from joining fundraising walks, to offering professional expertise, to not-for-profit organizations. A good friend of mine who is a tax accountant, for example, helps elderly people fill out their tax forms at a local senior citizen center. Taking the position of Captain of a fundraising walk is also a great way to raise your profile in the company.

If you are the parent of school-aged children, then you are probably well aware of the numerous volunteering opportunities available, including tutoring, and fundraising activities like bake sales and seasonal events. In this age of tight school budgets, most educational institutions are happy to welcome volunteer help. And the advantages for you: an opportunity to make contact with other parents and a chance to learn more about what is going on at your child's school.

There are also volunteer opportunities with organizations that serve young people, like the Boy and Girl Scouts, Big Brothers and Big Sisters, to name a few.

Neighborhood clean-ups, tree plantings and block parties are all enjoyable activities that benefit your immediate environment, and also offer excellent net-working opportunities.

If you enjoy the outdoors, volunteering with organizations that do trash cleanups on beaches, or work to maintain walking or riding trails, would be in tune with your personal interests. It is also a way to meet people who share a common interest with you, as well as offering networking opportunities. Moreover, if you are really adventurous, you can join a volunteering project in another part of the country, or even in another part of the world. This will be yet another priceless opportunity to expand both your realm of experiences and your network.

If politics is your bag, there are numerous volunteering and networking opportunities to be had at all levels. This can range from addressing a local issue, like electing a candidate to your local school board, to nationwide elections. Political campaigns are extremely labor intensive: people are always needed to stuff envelopes, make calls, and make the personal contacts that are often key to successful campaigns and candidacies. Along with the chance to further your favorite candidate or cause, you can also take advantage of the many opportunities to expand your network with people who share your political views.

From Local Giving to a Global Payoff

Bonnie Ross-Parker's Story: *I love to network. For me, networking is no different than a stroll along the beach. Just like looking for an unusual shell or stone, I love the anticipation of who I might meet or the relationship I might create. Networking is my version of a treasure hunt. I like to look for and uncover the unexpected. It was during an after-hours networking event that I met an unexpected treasure. I began a conversation with a young woman who was the program director for the Junior Chamber of Commerce of Atlanta. At the time I was looking for new avenues to speak and sell my products, and she was looking for new speakers. When I shared that my expertise was networking, she was eager to book me on the Chamber calendar. I asked about their budget to pay speakers. She was quick to tell me that they rely totally on the generosity of community talent. I remembered that you never know what can come from an act of generosity, and I did not have anything scheduled at the time, so I accepted the invitation to speak.*

As it turned out, I began feeling enthusiastic about my commitment. I imagined 60-75 young professionals eager to learn new networking ideas! Enlightening them early in their careers was certainly worth my time and effort. After dinner I spoke for about half an hour, followed by a Q & A. Participants were respectful, asked great questions and expressed appreciation for my program.

When the formal part of the evening was over, I anticipated one-on-one interaction and book sales. To my disappointment I only sold two or three copies of my book "Walk in my Boots: The Joy of Connecting", and very few members approached me afterward to chat. The major exodus was to the cash bar inside. The program director came by, however, purchased a book and thanked me for what she felt was a "great presentation." She then told me she hoped the opportunity would present itself for her to return the favor. I felt the connection we made. She had counted on me and I had kept my commitment. Of course, I sent her a written thank you note.

It was several month's later when I heard from her. She had given my name to a woman in Nuremberg, Germany who had contacted the Chamber looking for a suggestion of someone with networking expertise to speak at an upcoming women's conference. I couldn't believe it! Talk about making a connection count! Three days later I got a call from the director of the German conference. She had already visited my website, repeated the glowing testimonial she had received, and wanted to check on my availability. Within a short time I agreed to her very generous terms and a contract was signed. You never know what can happen unless you make every connection count. My keynote speech in Germany is a powerful example of the opportunities that can result from volunteering your time.

Exercise: *Finding That Volunteering Opportunity*

It is important to volunteer in an area you are interested in, and to be sincere. If you are only volunteering for the networking opportunities, it will soon become obvious, and work against you. In this exercise, first jot down some areas of interest, or causes you would be interested in helping:

Look around, in your neighborhood, your local news-paper, or online, and write down two or three volunteer opportunities that you think would be in tune with your interests and concerns, along with the contact phone numbers.

Finally, pick the one or two that resonate the strongest with you, then make that phone call and get involved. I assure you that if you participate fully and sincerely, before you know it, viable networking opportunities will begin to appear.

Now that you have studied some of the principles of Formal, Targeted Networking, it is time for you to create your own Networking Plan. You will need to know what it is you want to accomplish, and have identified the particular organization that can help you reach those goals. Having decided that, you will need to devise a plan for how to access this "hard to reach" person.

Exercise: *Creating a Networking Plan*

Define your goals:

- What do I want to do?

- Where do I want to be?

Once you have thought this through, answer the following questions:

- Who has the power or authority to help make this happen?

- Who has access to this person (or these people)?

As a final step, contact the above "access people" and put the wheels for networking in motion.

Chapter 11
Follow-up, The Key to Collaboration

Without follow-up, that great connection, great conversation, and great potential will be a great waste!

— Nadia Bilchik

Professional practitioners of the art of networking emphasize that *follow-up* is the most important element. "Eighty percent of networking is following up," says Rick Frishman co-author with Jill Lublin of *Networking Magic*. "Don't let relationships languish until you need something," he says. "That's mooching, not networking."

Revisiting The Time Factor

You may recall my comment that fear, more often than time, is what stops most people from networking. Still, I do recognize that many of us have to deal with a time crunch. Nevertheless, responding to someone's e-mail, sending someone an article of interest, inquiring about someone's health, or following up on finding a telephone number for someone, does not take up a lot of time. Also, you can be strategic about this. Once you have invested time in expanding your social network, you can methodically map out the most important individuals for you to invest in further.

And if you truly accept the importance of networking for your professional and personal future, you will set aside the time. One professional I know blocks out about four hours a week on her calendar to spend adding people to her database, updating entries, and sending e-mail. She also attends at least one event a week. Another individual who works in public relations, the ultimate networking job, sets aside a day twice a year to update and reorganize his database of 5,000 names.

In life we find time for what we think of as important. Once you see that networking to build mutually beneficial relationships is a survival tool, you will make a point to set aside the time. Truly, it is the best survival tool we have in dealing with change; it is our most precious safety net. The tip here is to make this an automatic part of your life, and not to see this as a separate time-consuming event.

PLUGGING IN TO CYBER-NETWORKS

Cyberspace, if it is used properly, can help you make very efficient use of your time. As we all know, the Internet plays an increasingly important role in our lives. The tipping point probably came in 1997, when consumers bought more computers than automobiles. It's hard to believe, but just three years later, in 2000, worldwide personal computer sales overtook the number of television sets sold yearly!

Not surprisingly, if you consider the proliferation of all kinds of interest groups, newsgroups and blogs, as well as the ability of e-mail to reconnect you with friends you last wrote a letter to five years ago, cyberspace is where a lot of social networking is taking place right now. In the age of virtual communication, follow-up has never been easier or quicker. No longer do we have to write a thank you note, find a stamp and make sure we pass a post office. It is now as easy as a couple of clicks.

So, what constitutes meaningful cyber-networking? *Expert Networkers* use all of the communications media at their disposal: including landlines, cellular telephones, voice mail, conference calls, fax, video-conferencing, pagers, e-mail, and e-mail attachments.

A simple "thank you" e-mail to the person you met yesterday telling them about a Press Club meeting that may be of interest to them, or a support group that focuses on single moms is polite, useful, and effective. If you make sure that your e-mail is short, gracious and specific, you cannot go wrong. The other good news is that if for any reason they don't reply, you are not dealing with rejection face to face.

But be careful how you use these new media. Long, multi-forwarded e-mails tend to be irritating and only in rare cases do they serve as good follow-up. Cyber-networking is not about forwarding those terminally long, "cute" e-mail attachments, or the endless jokes that are always making the rounds.

In addition, be careful with how you use your e-mailing list. If you are sending out a friendly e-mail to a group, make a point of hiding the fact by choosing the "blind copy" option. That way, all of the group's e-mail addresses will not appear. Otherwise, it will look thoughtless to a relative stranger to see a long list of e-mail addresses at the top of the message.

Put the action or topic of your e-mail in the subject line so the recipient will know that it is not spam. And be sure you personalize your message. People are dealing with electronic overload so be specific, be conscious of their time, and always check for spelling errors before you hit "Send." Finally, cyber communication is a wonderful tool that you should take care not to abuse. Do not use it *in place* of face-to-face communication. Face-to-face is incrementally more impacting and powerful.

Follow Up with A Suggestion or Recommendation

One way I have found to be very beneficial in creating rapport is to send articles or information that you think could be of interest to that particular person. Telling a new contact about a good restaurant that you just found, a great book you recently read, or a movie you recommend, are all good examples of helpful follow-up.

Bonne Nardi studied successful networkers who have truly adapted to the new, less structured work environment. She found that to keep their network engines revved, workers constantly attend to three tasks:

- building a network

- adding new people to it, and

- maintaining it.

Of the three, Nardi found that maintenance was the most important task. According to Nardi, "NetWORK is an ongoing process of keeping a personal network in good repair. In the words of one study participant, 'Relationships are managed and fed over time, much as plants are.'"

The people Nardi interviewed emphasized the importance of keeping contacts happy and feeling taken care of. They emphasized that small, personal touches, such as taking people to the most fashionable restaurant, or playing a round of golf with them, yielded out of proportion rewards.

NETWORK MAINTENANCE AS AN ART AND A SCIENCE

True networking professionals can be very systematic about the essential task of network maintenance. Nardi gave the example of one individual who, as a public relations executive for a large telecommunications company, is a networking professional. It is certainly instructive to observe how he goes about "feeding and maintaining" his network:

"You manage it. It really is a planned program of activities. It's a variety of different communications and different forms over time, from calling, sending a fax, something to read, arranging a meeting with the person who is the senior executive. It's offering a theater ticket, inviting someone to a seminar, sending an advance copy of a particular report, and when you have a major announcement, calling them first. Remembering their wife's or their husband's name, understanding what their hobbies are. If one of these people builds canoes and you come across an article about canoe building, you send it to them. In many different ways, it's demonstrating an understanding of who they are and what they're interested in."

Vlad Bog, who is head of Human Resources for the Coca-Cola Company in Romania, is equally systematic. At a recent Networking for Success seminar in Bucharest, he described how he goes about network maintenance. Vlad said that he has divided his network into several different categories. For example, his networks are:

- Close family

- Skiing buddies

- Colleagues

- Coca-Cola Bottlers

- Agencies

- Parents of his children's friends

- Old school friends

- Golf buddies

- Former colleagues

- U.S. colleagues

He then prioritizes which people in each group require regular contact. Let's call this our "primary network," the people who have earned more of our energy and time. Vlad then very consciously decides on the type of communication he is going to use to maintain the relationship. For example, to stay in touch with certain ski buddies, he will send a recent article on special skiing deals that he may have come across in a magazine or newspaper.

For business contacts in the bottlers' category, he may e-mail weekly updates on sales, or new trends in the bottling industry.

The key to this technique is to be very specific in what you send. Then, people will see that you have taken the time, without being asked, to take their special interests into account.

Dedicated *Expert Networkers* keep files about their contacts' birthdays, favorite candies or drinks, any tidbit that may be used to deliver a personalized gift or message. One individual even takes along her list of top 20 contacts when she travels, and sends postcards. Another writes personal letters to his contacts several times a year, trying to pick holidays like Thanksgiving, when his notes won't be lost in a pile of mail.

In one very high-tech solution, someone I know has developed a computer database that beeps after specified intervals to alert him to the fact that he had not called a contact in the database.

Expert Networkers are also very clear that there is such a thing as too much communication with your network. You also have to avoid being a pest. Communicate when you have something of value to offer, or when you have something genuine to share. Don't just spam out "Hello, how are you?" notes.

Remember, it is important to follow up in a non-threatening way and always be sure to say "Thank You." Also, don't make the "911 call" to somebody you haven't been in regular contact with. It creates too much pressure. Save these types of requests for people you've kept in touch with and you already have a mutually beneficial relationship.

Nadia Bilchik

Exercise: *Maintaining Your Networking Relationships*

Think carefully about all the people in your life—both at work and those who you know socially. Categorize them into at least six groups (or more if you wish) and enter their names below:

Group 1. CATEGORY: _____ / NAMES:

Group 2. CATEGORY: _____ / NAMES:

Group 3. CATEGORY: _____ / NAMES:

Group 4. CATEGORY: _____ / NAMES:

Group 5. CATEGORY: _____ / NAMES:

Group 6. CATEGORY: _____ / NAMES:

Go over the names you wrote and circle the "primary" people in each group.

Now, brainstorm with a friend or colleague as to the different ways you could stay in touch. It may be something extravagant like sending football tickets with prime seating to a key client. Or, it could be as simple as an e-mailed birthday acknowledgement. But, whatever you do—do it with a sense of creativity and originality.

How Do You Follow Up With Non-Reciprocators?

There are cases where some individuals become disenchanted with the whole process. For example, one of my friends complained, "I invest and invest and invest. I give and I'm kind, and it never comes back."

One part of the answer is patience. It might take a year, and it will most likely take a lot longer than you expect. But there is also nothing wrong with reminding certain individuals of the favor you performed—as long as you do it tactfully. You could say, "I'm so pleased I was able to help you on that project; you've done so well; and I've got an issue now and I was wondering how you'd suggest I proceed?"

Sometimes people just aren't conscious. We tend to think people are psychic. We like to think they know they should do the right thing. But sometimes you actually have to ask. However, you won't be pushy if you ask in the right way and phrase it correctly. When you ask somebody for their assistance, give them an option. For example: "Cliff, you have been very successful in the publishing industry. Would you be able to give me a few suggestions on how to get started?"

Just as long as it does not seem that the other party feels they are "entitled," you will find that most people truly enjoy helping other people.

CHAPTER 12

BECOMING A NETWORKING "GO-TO" PERSON

If someone listens or stretches out a hand, or whispers a kind word of encouragement, or attempts to understand another person, extraordinary things can start to happen.

— Loretta Girzartis

How would you like to become widely recognized as an *Expert Networker*? Here's the trick: you will not only make the suggestion of introducing two people to each other who could benefit from a meeting, you will actually go ahead and set up the meeting.

This is how you become what Zig Ziglar describes as a networking GO-TO person. Networking experts, Robert Littell and Donna Fisher, describe it as "NetWeaving." In all of these cases, you are practicing an altruistic "win-win" form of networking in which you concentrate on WIFY (What's In it For YOU?) rather than WIFM (What's In it For ME?) According to Littell, one of the developers of the Pay It Forward concept, NetWeaving works in accordance with the Golden Rule of doing for others as you would want them to do for you. But the assumption, as in golden, is that being generous will have its own rewards.

A Go-To Person in Action

Debra's Story: *Several months ago, I received an e-mail from a woman, Jessica, referring in the subject line to a young fashion designer who I'd interviewed a couple years earlier. Jessica, a special projects editor at a national teen magazine, was writing to me upon the suggestion of our mutual friend to let me know about her upcoming book, a collection of Latin-inspired entertaining tips and recipes. I corresponded with Jessica over e-mail, then passed along her book information to the appropriate editor and our magazine ended up doing a small feature on the book.*

Fast forward a few months, and I get a call to do an appearance on ABC's The View. Accompanying me on the trip was a colleague, Madeleine, who is an art director and was helping to style the segment. Madeleine and I often bounced career ideas off one another, and she mentioned that while in New York for The View appearance she would try to do some informational

---

interviewing; she was considering moving to New York to work at a national magazine. I offered to e-mail Jessica — who I had never met, really barely knew and had e-mailed with just a few times — on the off chance that she might be willing to hook Madeleine up to meet with some art directors at her magazine. Jessica agreed wholeheartedly.

It turns out, Madeleine and Jessica had gone to the same high school in Atlanta, just several years apart! When Madeleine arrived at the magazine, Jessica greeted her with open arms and ushered her into meetings with the magazine's creative director and other senior art directors. After looking at Madeleine's portfolio, the creative director warmly provided her with a list of names of other magazines that should see her.

This set off a series of excellent informational and job interviews for Madeleine. She just recently accepted a fabulous senior art director position with a top fashion magazine. Who knew my one little e-mail to someone I'd never met could open such doors for a friend of mine?

When you set out to become a Networking Go-To Person for other people, you need to answer two key questions:

1) How can I put OTHER people together into win-win relationships?

The giver does this without expecting anything in return, but has the confidence that benevolence of this kind is often rewarded later on, and often in unexpectedly wonderful ways.

2) How can I act as a "resource provider" for someone else?

This is accomplished either by serving in that role yourself, or by offering others access to your extended network of contacts, including people and information.

The benefit is that you become a Strategic Resource. It is a powerful position to be in. Instead of being the person in need, you're the person in charge. You're the arranger. It's like becoming the host/hostess, as I described earlier, in casual networking.

When someone at CNN asks me for the number of the Sri Lankan Ambassador, I may not know it offhand, but I make the effort to find it for them. I know with certainty that I will be calling that very same person at some point for assistance. If I have followed up, the chances of them assisting me go up incrementally.

How do you become this kind of three-dimensional person, who is known by name as a strategic resource— the person recognized as a generous individual who has invested in his or her network, or organization?

- Try to meet face-to-face when possible.

- Most people are receptive, but you should always confirm that they are (do not push if you notice reluctance).

- Never make assumptions, get all the facts before moving ahead (feel the person out and ask qualifying questions).

- Find common ground (by determining what their personal interests are).

- Humanize the person and the conversation (do not be judgmental, try to see the world from their viewpoint).

- Create value by first making the mental connections and then following through (send an e-mail that relates to their personal interests).

Exercise: *Being a Networking GO-TO Person*

Think of a friend or a co-worker who you know relatively well. List what you know of their work, their hobbies, their interests.

Make mental connections on where you have common ground, and come up with suggestions of any resources or guidance you can offer, if appropriate.

Finally, contact that person via phone or e-mail with your suggestion. Now, expand this exercise out to other people in your network.

In some cases, you may not have anything to offer. That's fine. An *Expert Networker* knows when to be helpful, but also knows when to pull back. If this is a person you would like to make a connection with at another point, you can be helpful in a more subtle way. For example…

The parent of one of my daughter's classmates is the director of a downtown theater. While I was downtown running personal errands one day, I came across a particularly inviting and pleasant bistro. Later that day, I sent a friendly and very well received little e-mail telling her about my "find." I am now identified to this theater director as the "go-to" person for downtown information.

This is a valuable exercise, so even if you do not have a real-life scenario, make one up. You'll find that even if you have nothing to offer immediately, the opportunities will eventually present themselves. The important thing is that you have set out with the intention of becoming a go-to networker.

Also make sure that once you have found what works for you, that you always *follow up*. It sounds easy, but it is the one part of networking where most people slip up.

EXPERT NETWORKING

I am living proof that *Expert Networking* WORKS, that building mutually beneficial relationships is one of the *best* ways to survive and thrive both personally and professionally. Therefore I strongly urge you to get started NOW.

Apply these simple principles.

- Focus on exuding Positive Energy.

- Have an open, friendly, giving attitude.

- Create opportunities to connect and take advantage of them.

- Make sure your networking is mutually beneficial.

- Actively participate in a forum of your choice, and most important,

- Follow up with ease and sincerity.

If you adhere to this formula, you will have a more fulfilling, successful and ultimately profitable life, as you will observe in this personal story:

Networking as a Life Enhancing Skill

Ney's Story: *If "Necessity is the mother of invention" then "using every trick in the book" is its daughter! Or so I have come to believe as I review the obstacles and "ladders" that I have used to achieve the contented and fulfilled life I now lead. Paramount among my "ladders" has been the application of what is today called "networking." Mine has been an unlikely sojourn through contemporary American life both public and private, and it is my collection of people, who, through their presences in my daily life to varying degrees and intensity, have made the trip an adventure and remarkable in the destinations to which I have arrived and continue to anticipate.*

Leaving a small rural Northern Virginia hamlet populated with a family and community steeped in the mores and conventions of post war, mid-century attitudes, I headed for the big city of Philadelphia to seek an education and a future. My first network of friends was as wide and varied as the distance in space and culture I had just traveled. I lived in a hostel for young ladies run by Dominican Nuns. Little did I know that within the corridors of the "Lucy Eaton Smith Residence for Young Ladies" was as wild and radical a group of women as I was to ever encounter. Women of all ages, from all parts of the world had come to reside with the Sisters. All, like myself, were seeking to prepare for the next stage of our lives. I found myself exposed to girls whose rooms were grand salons of music, poetry and the arts, or simple holes in the wall where some girl or woman was hiding out from abuse, adultery, or abortion.

For three years I used my room as a base from which to foray out into various areas of the city, my destination determined only by the fellow resident who accompanied and exposed or guided me. They showed me how to ride a bus, take a taxi or jump a turnstile. Through them I learned to eat sushi, tamales, borscht, pierogies, and even what it meant to keep Kosher.

During the next 40 years as I traveled, worked and lived all over this country, I have sought to duplicate the complexity and diversity of that network of friends. I remained open to all who crossed my path. And whether it was big city or small town, I have eagerly introduced myself to the neighbors, garbage man, postman, and dry cleaners as well as having arrived at my new home with letters of introduction to the most elite of its inhabitants. I have never felt alone or out of place. I have celebrated almost every holiday known to man, and have been embraced and remembered in the prayers of people of every possible religious persuasion. And though never married, I am special aunt or godmother to children of all races and creeds and an extended family member to every tribe or nationality that inhabits this great melting pot.

> *I have long espoused the benefits of being open to the treasures available from the most unlikely hands and the affection and joy to be found in relationships with those who on first glance appear to be so different from ourselves. I have found networking to be most rewarding when utilized as a lifestyle rather than a technique. And I have found it to be most effective when one participates not trying to identify what is "on offer" from the other but confident in the realization that all others offer us new sets of relationships and encounters, each possessing riches of information or experience.*

As a reminder, always strive to do the following:

N - be **Natural**

E - show **Enthusiasm**

T - display **Tenacity**

W - **Win** everyone over with your positive attitude

O - see a possible networking **Opportunit**y in every situation

R - be **Relaxed**

K - share your **Knowledg**e

I - show genuine **Interest**

N - take **No** one for granted

G - be **Generous** and **Giving**

As I've noted many times, networking has become my passion. Applying the lessons of this book to my own life has enabled me to make an extremely successful transition from one country to another. It has also allowed me to vastly expand my career horizons, and most importantly, to make meaningful and generous connections with a vast array of wonderful people. If you have read this book closely, and mindfully followed the exercises, you too will now be in the position to become a generous, engaged and successful *Expert Networker*, with powerful skills that will enhance all aspects of your life.

BIBLIOGRAPHY

Allessandro, Tony (2000). *Charisma: Seven Keys to Developing the Magnetism That Leads to Success.* Warner Books, Inc.

Brown, S.L.; Nesse, R.M.; Vinokur, A.D.; & Smith, D.M. (2003) Providing social support may be more beneficial than receiving it: results from a prospective study of mortality. *Psychological Science*, 14 (4): pp 320-327

Canfield, Jack; Hansen, Mark Victor; L. Ruttel, Martin; Rogerson, Maida, (2001). *Chicken Soup for the Soul at Work.* Health Communications, Inc.

Carnegie, Dale; & Pell, Arthur Ed. (1990). *How to Win Friends and Influence People.* Simon and Schuster Adult Publishing Group.

Chopra, Deepak (1995). *Seven Spiritual Laws of Success: A Practical Guide to the Fulfillment of Your Dreams.* Amber-Allen Publishing.

Eisenberger, N. I.; & Lieberman, M. D. (2004). Why rejection hurts: a common neural alarm system for physical and social pain. *Trends in Cognitive Sciences,* 8, pp 294-300.

Eng, Patricia M.; Rimmi, Eric B.; Fitzmaurice, Garrett; & Kawachi, Ichiro (2002). Social ties and change in social ties in relation to subsequent total and cause-specific mortality and coronary heart disease incidence in men. *American Journal of Epidemiology,* 155 (8), pp 700-709.

Erickson, Bonnie (2003). Social networks: The value of variety. *Contexts: Understanding people in their social worlds.* 2(1) Retrieved from: http://www.contextsmagazine.org/content_sample_v2-1.php

Ferrazzi, Keith; & Raz, Tahl (2005). *Never Eat Alone: And Other Secrets to Success, One Relationship at a Time.* Doubleday Publishing.

Frishman, Rick; Lublin, Jill; & Steisel, Mark (2004). *Networking Magic: Find the Best — from Doctors, Lawyers, and Accountants, to Homes, Schools and Jobs.* Adams Media Corporation.

Futch, Ken (2005). *Take Your Best Shot: Turning Situations Into Opportunities.* Wagrub Press.

Goleman, Daniel (2002). *Working with Emotional Intelligence*. Bantam Books.

Goleman, Daniel (2005). *Emotional Intelligence*. Bantam Books.

Granovetter, M.S. (1973) The Strength of Weak Ties. *American Journal of Sociology*, 6: 1360-1380

Hansen, Kristin A. (2001, January 18). Geographical Mobility. *US Census Bureau*. Retrieved from: http://www.census.gov

Healy, Melissa (2005). Girlfriends: They may promote health. *The Los Angeles Times*, May 26, 2005.

Kehoe, John (1997). *Mind Power into the 21st Century. Techniques for Success and Happiness*. Zoetic Books.

Klaus, Peggy (2004). Brag!: *The Art of Tooting Your Own Horn Without Blowing It*. Warner Business.

Lin, Nan (2001). Building a theory of Social Capital. *In Social Capital, Theory and Research*. N. Lin; K.S. Cook; R.S. Burd. New York, Aldine de Gruyter, pp 3-30.

Littell, Robert S.; & Fisher, Donna (2001). *Power Netweaving: 10 Secrets to Successful Relationship Marketing*. National Underwriting Company.

Mackay, Harvey B. (2005). *Swim with the Sharks Without Being Eaten Alive*. HarperCollins Publishers.

Mackay, Harvey B. (1999). *Dig Your Well Before You're Thirsty: The Only Networking Book You'll Ever Need*. Doubleday Publishing.

Nardi, Bonnie A.; Whittaker, Steve; & Schwarz, Heinrich (2000). It's Not What You Know, It's Who You Know: Work in the Information Age. *First Monday: A Peer-Reviewed Journal on the Internet*. Retrieved from: http://www.firstmonday.org/issues/issue5_5/nardi/

RoAne, Susan (2000). *How to Work a Room: The Ultimate Guide to Savvy Socializing in Person and Online*. HarperCollins Publishers.

Robbins, Anthony; Mcclendon, Joseph; Anfuso, Dominick V. (2006). *Inner Strength: Harnessing the Power of Your Six Primal Needs*. The Free Press.

Robbins, Anthony (1992). *Awaken the Giant Within: How to Take Immediate Control of Your Mental, Emotional, Physical and Financial Destiny*. Simon and Schuster Adult Publishing Group.

Ruiz, Don Miguel (1997). *The Four Agreements*. Amber-Allen Publishing.

Rutledge, Thomas; Reis, Steven E.; Olson, Marian; Owens, Jane; Kelsey, Shertl F.; Pepine, Carl J.; Manka, Sunil; Rogers, William J.; Bairey Merz, C. Noel; Sopko, Goerge; Cornell, Carol E.; Sharaf, Barry; & Matthews, Karen A. (2004). Social networks are associated with lower mortality rates among women with suspected coronary disease: The National Heart, Lung, and Blood Institute-sponsored Women's Ischemia Syndrome Evaluation Study. *Psychosomatic Medicine*, 66:pp 882-888.

Siebert, Scott E.; Kraimer, Maria L.; & Liden, Robert C. (2001). A Social Capital Theory of Career Success. *Academy of Management Journal*.

Silk, Joan B.; Alberts, Susan C.; & Altmann, Jeanne (2003). Social bonds of female baboons enhance infant survival. *Science*, Volume 302, Number 5648, pp 1231-1234.

Swanbrow, Diane (1998). To retire well, invest in making friends. *Eurekalert!* Retrieved from: http://www.eurkealert.org

Ziglar, Zig (2000). *See You at the Top*. Pelican Publishing Company, Inc.

– NOTES –

- NOTES -

– NOTES –

– NOTES –

– NOTES –

Printed in the United States
151328LV00002B/78/A

9 781425 937676